1. Heerpaucken. 2. Soldaten Trummeln. 3. Schweitzer Pfeifflin 4. Amboß

The World of Baroque & Classical Musical Instruments

for Gwen

Proverbs 31, 10-31

By the same author
Already published
The World of Medieval & Renaissance Musical Instruments

In preparation
The World of Romantic & Modern Musical Instruments
The World of Ethnographic Musical Instruments

'The Mozart Family', anonymous, *c.* 1770. Maria Anna
(Nannerl), square piano; Wolfgang Amadeus, violin;
Leopold, bass lute, probably a theorbo (note the open
bass strings running beside the fingerboard). (*Stadtarchiv,
Augsburg*)

The World of Baroque & Classical Musical Instruments

Jeremy Montagu

The Overlook Press
Woodstock   New York

First published in the United States in 1979
by The Overlook Press, Lewis Hollow Road,
Woodstock, New York 12498

Copyright © Jeremy P. S. Montagu 1979

Library of Congress Cataloging in Publication Data
Montagu, Jeremy.
The world of baroque and classical musical instruments.
   Continues The world of medieval and renaissance
   musical instruments.
   Bibliography: p.
   Includes index.
   1. Musical instruments
   I. Title
ML465.M65   781.9′1′0903   78 65227
   ISBN 0 87951 089 7

Printed in Great Britain

Contents

Colour Plates

Black and White Plates

Text Figures

All photographs not otherwise acknowledged are those of the institutions or persons named

Preface

The period covered by this book is approximately from 1600 to 1800. This is an era which can be divided in a number of different ways and various names can be used for each section. Such division is never easy and the separate sections can never be watertight. For example, it is obvious that the baroque period continued at least until the death in 1750 of its greatest master, J. S. Bach, but by that date his sons had for some years already been writing in the style which is sometimes called rococo and sometimes pre-classical. Since our concern here is with the musical instruments, it has seemed simplest to divide the book into three chapters to correspond to the three most important sections of this period. The first we call the Early Baroque, beginning in about 1600 and ending somewhere late in the seventeenth century—a phrase which is deliberately vague—and in it we describe the instrumentarium with which our period began, continuing from where the previous book, *The World of Medieval & Renaissance Musical Instruments*, ended. The second period is the High Baroque, which runs from somewhere in the latter part of the seventeenth century to about 1750, in which we can examine the great changes which took place as those instruments which had survived from the Renaissance were transformed into those of the Baroque. The third is that period which, for simplicity, we call Classical and in which we include what some may prefer to call the pre-classical, because the mould of the baroque was already broken and the styles of the classical were clearly adumbrated. This is the period in which the next great change of instrumental style and technology took place, and which saw the beginnings of the symphony orchestra of the masters of the nineteenth century. That century and our own will be the subjects of a future volume.

Introduction

Music is the most ephemeral of the arts, for it consists of the orderly arrangement of sounds and once the sound has ceased, the music has passed beyond recall, save in the memories of the hearers. Musical notation was invented as an attempt to give permanence to what is essentially evanescent, but it is no more than an *aide-mémoire*, a skeleton which the performer may clothe with flesh drawn from his imagination or from his memory of other performances. None of the world's cultures which have devised notations have invented any way of indicating the tone-quality of the sounds desired. The notes of the scale are recorded though not their precise pitch, for the tuning or temperament to be used is seldom if ever specified. Their duration and their loudness are very vaguely indicated and, in the really high musical cultures such as the Chinese, the way in which the sounds are to be produced is noted, the manner of striking and fingering the strings of the lute or the zither. In Europe there has never been so precise a notation and only in the memories of performers and teachers does anything survive even of late nineteenth century performance style. 'When Clara Schumann taught me, she played the piece in this way', said one of her surviving pupils, and there are few people today who can remember the sonorities of an orchestra conducted by Brahms. Indeed, even with the marvels of modern technology we are unsure of the tone qualities of instruments in common use forty years ago, and the constraints of 'fitting it into a side' leave us uncertain of the normal performance speeds of those who recorded music before the days of magnetic tape and of long-playing discs. Thus, dependent as we are on our fallible memories of music that we heard so short a time ago, it is obvious that we have no real idea of what sounds the earlier masters heard when they wrote the works which have come down to us. We must never forget that a composer hears his music in his mind; it does not come to him as dots on paper but as sounds created by instruments and voices. Instruments change over the years, as do instrumental and vocal techniques, and when we hear baroque and classical music played by the modern symphony orchestra, sung by our great choral societies, and played and sung by modern soloists and chamber groups, we are hearing a travesty of the composer's original intentions. It is precisely as though the National Gallery were to display new versions by modern artists of paintings by the old masters instead of the originals.

It is the purpose of books such as this to try to show something of the instruments of past ages and to attempt, so far as it can be done in words, to indicate something of the sounds with which the great composers of the past clothed their music. Those who wish to hear the true sounds of the music of earlier times must seek out the growing number of ensembles which, by using surviving original instruments or accurate reproductions of such instruments, are trying to recreate the original sonorities. They should, however, be wary of those ensembles that play both Bach and Mozart, both Handel and Haydn upon the same instruments, for, as will become apparent in these pages, not one single instrument used by Johann Sebastian Bach would have been tolerated in an orchestra directed by his son's pupil, Wolfgang Amadeus Mozart, nor would Bach have tolerated any of the instruments used by Heinrich Schütz. There is a tendency today to think that an old instrument is old and to forget the continual changes of technique, style and taste which separate the generations and which should compel us to ask 'But *how* old is it?' Every generation had its own preferred sound, as did every geographical cultural area; Bach in Leipzig and Handel in London were working in quite different sonorities, and even more different were the sonorities heard by Bach in Leipzig in 1740 from those heard at the first concerts in the Leipzig Gewandhaus in 1781.

Looking back from the twentieth century one has the impression that the period covered by this book is striped with bands of alternate development and rest. The first half or three-quarters of the seventeenth century appears to show little change from the instruments that we have already encountered at the end of the sixteenth century, perhaps because most of Europe was occupied with other matters which compelled more attention. In Britain the Tudor/Jacobean period was dissolving into religious and political unrest and civil war. France, until Louis XIV attained his majority in the middle of the century, was unstable and restless. Central Europe, the German States and Austria and Bohemia were embroiled in thirty years of continuous warfare. Spain, sated with the gold of the Americas and exhausted by the struggle in the Low Countries, was sinking into cultural lethargy. Only Italy was comparatively at peace, and this is reflected in the musical and organological history of this period.

As Europe became more settled in the middle of the century, attention could be spared for the arts and there ensued a period of violent change in which all the instruments surviving from the Renaissance were drastically altered, before the end of the century, into those of the baroque. These alterations particularly affected the woodwind instruments, changing their appearance, their sound and their capabilities in musical performance. This was followed by another period of comparative stability, with little change in instruments or in their use, until, in the next century, again in the latter part, another violent change ensued, in which the instruments of the Baroque gave way to those of the Classical period, with perhaps less alteration to the woodwind but with far more to the keyboards, brass and strings.

It may be that this impression is quite false, and that changes were going on quietly and gradually all the time, as they have been doing in our own lifetime. Just as a close examination of a pointillist painting shows only a mass of spots of different colours whereas a retreat to a more distant view suddenly reveals patterns and shapes, so the gradual changes in instruments and in their sonorities, hardly noticed as such by their contemporaries, can be seen by us to coalesce, so that we see patterns which may not have been apparent and which may not have been significant in their own time. Nevertheless, to us those patterns are there and, with hindsight, they seem to be important for it is their results which control the sound of music. It is only by studying them, by studying the instruments, which were the tools of each musical style, and their sonorities that we can be aware of the materials with which the great composers constructed their musical edifices.

Chapter I

The Early Baroque

We left *The World of Medieval & Renaissance Musical Instruments* with the beginnings of the orchestra, with the band of players that Monteverdi specified in the score of his opera *L'Orfeo*, first performed in Mantua in 1607. It was in Italy at the beginning of the seventeenth century that the new styles of music were developing: the opera, the orchestra, the 'new music' of Caccini. It was also in Italy that the new family of violins, which was to serve as the basis of the orchestra for the next four hundred years, had come to perfection. Instruments made in the sixteenth century by masters such as Gasparo da Salò of Brescia and Andrea Amati of Cremona are still in use today, and the basic form of the violin family remains as it was established in the sixteenth century. Italy was also the main source for woodwind instruments in the early seventeenth century and for lutes of all sizes, though many of the lute makers were Germans and Austrians living in Italy. Harpsichords and clavichords came either from Italy or from the Low Countries, but it was not to be long before the main centre of keyboard making shifted to the north. The manufacture of brass instruments was still centred on Nuremberg and it is from Germany that we have the first great encyclopedia of musical instruments, 'De Organographia', the second volume of Michael Praetorius's *Syntagma Musicum*, published in Wolfenbüttel in 1619.

From the beginning of the seventeenth century onwards, more and more instruments survive in a sufficiently good condition for us to hear their sound and assess their musical use. Even when an instrument has been so 'restored' or otherwise falsified in periods when less was known about them and less care taken over authenticity than is generally agreed to be desirable today, sufficient often survives for it to be possible to make a convincing reconstruction that will give us at least a fair idea of the original sonority. However, some instruments referred to in the literature of the period have failed to survive and for

these especially, and for many details of all the instruments of the period, we fall back upon Praetorius's work. He begins with a classified list and continues with a description of all the instruments in use in his day. He gives much more space to the organ than to any other instrument, including a detailed description of each type of pipe, followed by a list of the registrations of a number of famous organs from the fourteenth century onwards up to his own time. The cases of a number of the organs he describes still survive but, with only one or two exceptions, the ravages of subsequent repairs and restorations have left little of the sounds that he might have heard. His book concludes with the famous 'Theatrum Instrumentorum' (see plates 2, 16, 18, 20, 21 and 22), which illustrates all the instruments that he describes and a number which do not appear in his text. These illustrations are of great importance today, both because no examples of some of the instruments have survived and because his illustrations are not only carefully drawn but are the first and, until the present century, the last to be provided with a scale. It is this scale that has allowed modern makers to produce reconstructions of a number of the vanished instruments and the only thing that one has to be careful about is the conversion of the Brunswick ell, which Praetorius used, into modern measurements. The foot in the scale, as Bessaraboff pointed out, is the equivalent of about $11\frac{1}{4}$ modern inches or 285.36mm compared with the modern foot of 304.79mm, and the inch is the equivalent of 23.78mm, which is somewhat smaller than the modern inch of 25.39mm. Praetorius was also the first to illustrate non-European instruments, although he often located them on the opposite side of the globe to their true place of origin; for example, the Indonesian gamelan instruments are said to be American, a Benin ivory horn is said to be Indian and an African drum is said to be Muscovite. However, many of the instruments are drawn with the same accuracy as the European instruments, as Klaus

Wachsmann has shown by comparing a surviving seventeenth century drum in the Ashmolean Museum at Oxford with the 'Muscovite' drum just referred to.

It is impossible to overestimate the importance of Praetorius's book. Of the later compilations such as Mersenne's *Harmonie Universelle*, which has rather more information about many of the instruments but illustrations that are far inferior in many respects, Talbot's manuscript, which has many detailed measurements but infuriating and frustrating lacunae, a small range and no illustrations, and Diderot and D'Alembert's *Encyclopédie*, with its detailed cross-sections of some instruments and minimal information on others, none has the range, the clarity of information and, above all, the scaled drawings of *Syntagma Musicum*.

Marin Mersenne was a very different sort of writer from Michael Praetorius. Praetorius was a professional musician, a *Kapellmeister* and a composer; Mersenne was a scholar and a philosopher and a considerable mathematician, with an enquiring interest into music and musical instruments, especially into their acoustics and other scientific aspects. His massive work, *Harmonie Universelle*, was published in Paris in 1636 and consists of an acoustical treatise, a study of music, counterpoint and composition, and finally a detailed treatise on all types of instruments with, as in Praetorius's book, special emphasis on the organ and, as one might expect with a physicist, special emphasis also on bells, instruments which have been studied by acousticians from the earliest times. He goes into far more detail than Praetorius about the instruments and how they are used, sometimes giving fingering charts, but he seldom gives any absolute measurements. He did insert some measured drawings into his own copy of the book, which was the master for the reprint by the Centre National de la Recherche Scientifique, and this modern edition is more valuable than copies of the original for all save bibliophiles, for Mersenne added many marginal comments and extra leaves, all of which include further information. His illustrations, however, range from the excellent to the crudest of rough sketches, as plate 1 will show. The viola da gamba to the left (the upper bridge is for a lyra da gamba) is drawn by his best artist, the pochette in the centre by a mediocre artist and the violin, if such it be, to the right is drawn by one of the worst, only excelled in incompetence by whoever drew some of the wind instruments. As a result, much of his textual information is extremely valuable, some of his illustrations are highly informative, and others merely leave us wondering what the instruments really looked like.

By the early seventeenth century it was becoming more common for composers to specify the instruments that they required for the performance of their music. Thus we have a fairly clear picture of their use, at least in the more formal music, though for many works we still have to guess what was required from hints and pay-sheets. Much informal music, however, especially dance music, was played on whatever instruments seemed suitable or were available. Sets of dance suites were published from the middle of the sixteenth century onwards either with a massive list of instruments covering all possible combinations or simply in four or five parts, leaving it to the players to sort out from among the instruments they had available which would play each line the best.

The music of the Church, especially in Italy, was quite another matter. Composers such as Giovanni Gabrieli had begun to specify the instruments that they required to accompany the music in St Mark's in Venice. The orchestra of St Mark's was by no means new but what was new was the indication on the music of specific orchestration and such experiments in contrasting tone colours as Gabrieli's 'Sonata pian'e forte'. Equally new were the subtle mixture of light and shade, a greater expressiveness, often a greater virtuosity of technique, the idea that the character of the music should follow the meaning of the words, and a greater range and flexibility of sonority: all were characteristic of the 'new music', whether religious or secular.

Thus the initial influences on the instruments of the Baroque were the opera, the Church and the new music itself.

Bowed String Instruments

The orchestra of the opera was predominantly one of bowed and plucked strings, numbering between half a dozen and a dozen in all. Many operas were written to be accompanied by such strings and keyboards alone and on the rare occasions that a larger orchestra of mixed instruments was employed, these remained the basic instruments. All operas, and also the allied dramatic entertainment the masque, included numerous dance sequences, a type of music for which viols were quite unsuited and for which the violins had been used ever since their invention. As a result there was a division among the bowed strings: viols were used for domestic and amateur music of the sort that today we would call chamber music, the early baroque equivalent of the string quartet, while violins were used by a far larger body of professional musicians, the ordinary orchestral players, as well as by the professional, semi-professional and amateur players of dance music at all levels of society. Throughout the period of this book many genre paintings, especially those of Dutch and Flemish painters, show scenes of music making which include violins far more often than viols. It is also a reflection of the less exalted place of the violin in the musical hierarchy that it is more often the violin than the viol which can be seen in the many allegorical paintings illustrating Vanitas (see, for example, plate XII in *The World of Medieval & Renaissance Musical Instruments*) and others of the Seven Deadly Sins.

The Viol

It was at this period that the viol was established in its best known form and many of the best makers were English. In Italy the viol had gone out of fashion save to play the bass lines in ensembles of other instruments and in Germany, too, it was much less used than before. In France, where the English viol was popular and much sought after, viols continued to be used and became important for virtuoso composers and performers. In England, conservative and old-fashioned in musical taste then as now, the viols playing in consorts remained a common and popular ensemble both for recreation by amateur performers and for listening to by audiences in court and castle. Public concerts in our sense of the term did not exist and music was played as incidental music for plays, as accompaniment to masques, in taverns and in private homes great and small. It was especially in the last of these that viols remained popular.

There were three basic sizes of viol: the treble, the tenor, which was a fourth or a fifth lower, and the bass, which was an octave lower than the treble

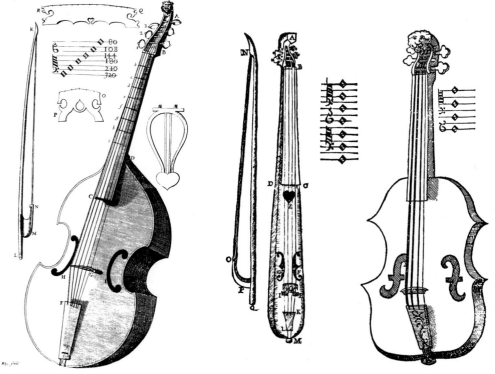

Plate 1 *Left to right:* viola da gamba with bow and bridge (bridge for lyra da gamba above), pochette and bow, violin. (*Marin Mersenne,* Harmonie Universelle, *Paris, 1636*)

1. 2. 3. Violn de Gamba. 4. Viol Bastarda. 5. Jtalianische Lyra de bracio.

(plate 2). Music was normally written for five or six viols, a common combination being one treble, two tenors and two basses, with a lute, organ or harpsichord. Other sizes of viol were sometimes used; the great bass or violone (see plate 22), which was tuned an octave below the tenor, was occasionally used in English consorts and in Italy as the bass for various groups and ensembles. There was also a great double bass, or contrabass viol or violone, tuned an octave below the bass viol, which doubled the bass line an octave lower but which seems to have been used comparatively rarely at this time. A small bass, the division viol, was used as a solo instrument since its slightly smaller size, with a consequent shorter stretch for the hand stopping the strings, made it easier to play elaborate divisions, as variations were known at this period. The name of the instrument in various languages can cause some slight confusion to the general reader, for in Italian the members of the family as a whole are called *viole da gamba* to distinguish them from the *viole da braccio* or violin family, but in English it has become customary to use that term in the singular, viola da gamba, for the bass viol and to call the other members of the family treble viol, tenor viol and so on, and to use

the word viol for the family as a whole. In France also the first part of the name, *viole*, is used for all the members of the family, whereas in Germany the second part of the name is used plurally for the family: *Gamben*. The chief characteristics of the family, as may be seen in plate I, are that all are held on or between the knees whereas only the larger violins were held in this way; that the neck is fretted; that the bow is usually held with the palm outwards so that the strong stroke is the up-bow, the pushing stroke, and not the down-bow, the pulling stroke; and, most important, that there were normally six strings and that these were tuned in fourths with a third in the middle, like those of the lute. The outline of the body varied quite widely, but that on the left of plate I was probably the commonest and the most typical. The belly of the viol is usually curved upwards in a smooth arch, neither as high nor as sharply arched as that of the violin, and the arch commences from the edges of the instrument, unlike that of the violin, which rises from a point some distance in from the edges. The back is normally flat and not arched, and it is broken at the shoulder so that the upper part of the body is less thick from front to back than the rest of it. The strings are attached to a tail-piece, which is usually hooked over a bar glued to the end of the instrument.

The soundboard or belly of the viols was thinner than that of the violins and the string tension lower, so that the sound was sweeter and with less projection. The strings used on both viols and violins, like those of the lute, were all of gut. The lower strings, which today are covered with thin wire to increase their mass, were made by taking several strands of gut and laying them up like a rope, which is why they were called catlines, from the name of a type of rope. The technique of making such strings has been very recently rediscovered by Djilda Abbott and Ephraim Segerman, and as yet we are only beginning to appreciate their tonal qualities. With such strings, there remains a perceptible tonal difference between the two families, for the sound of the violins is much louder and with much greater projection.

On the violin there is a marked tonal difference between the sound of a fingered note, when the vibrating length of the string is terminated by the soft flesh of the finger, and the sound of the open strings, when the length of the string is terminated by the hard edge of the nut, the bar at the top of the fingerboard. On the viols, because the string is stopped just behind a fret, the fret acts as another nut so that even with gut frets, which are softer than a wooden nut, there is less difference of tone between stopped and open strings; this homogeneity of tone quality is the most important function of the frets. As a result, there is more ringing resonance in the sound of the viol than in the violin, and this is increased by sympathetic resonance from the other strings, for the lighter construction of the body and the lower tension of the strings, as well as the greater number of strings available to add their resonance, increases the probability of resonance in sympathy with any note played. Violin strings are tuned a fifth apart and there was therefore a considerable difference between their thicknesses in order to obtain so great a difference of pitch with approximately the same tension; the strings of the viols, on the other hand, being tuned only a fourth or third apart, show much less difference in this respect and this again increases their blend of sonority.

In sum, the viol was a restrained instrument used mostly for polyphonic music, capable of intense emotion but always held-in within its compass; the violin, on the other hand, was brash and extrovert, gay or moody, used for entertainment music of all sorts. Neither was of itself inferior or superior to the other, but the course of music from the early seventeenth century onwards, and the desired sonority, went the way of the violin not that of the viol, so that from the latter part of the seventeenth century viols were less and less used in consort and little new music was written for such groups.

Among the other types of viol that were important was the lyra da gamba or lirone (plate 3). Its bridge, which can be seen at the top of plate 1 on the left, was much flatter than that of the ordinary viol, which can be seen below it, so that the player could easily bow on a number of strings simultaneously in order to play chords. The tuning, as can be seen from the table in Mersenne's illustration in plate 3, is re-entrant, as such zigzag tuning is called, and this also made it easy to play chords at the same time as the melody. It was thus an instrument designed for accompanying itself and, like all the Italian instruments with a name including the word *lyra*, it was thought of as the modern version of Apollo's lyre

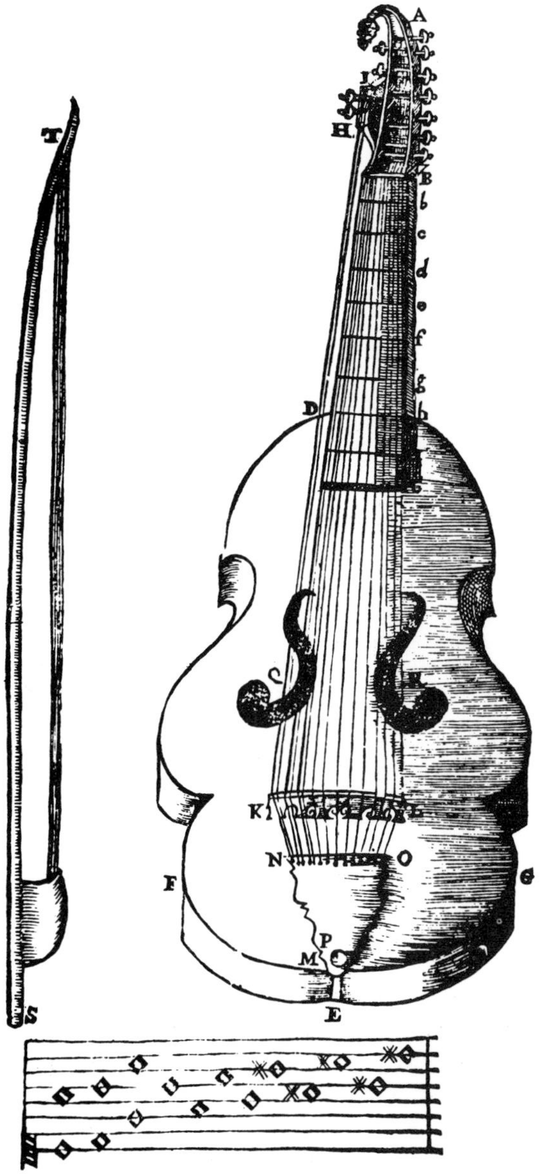

Plate 3   Lyra da gamba with bow and tuning schema. (*Mersenne*)

and the right instrument to accompany serious melodies and songs. Mersenne says, incidentally, that it is nothing like as difficult to tune as the great number of strings makes it appear and that one can, of course, tune it in all sorts of different ways to suit whatever is being played.

In England the ordinary bass viol was extensively used for chordal playing under the name of lyra viol. To make this technique easier, it was reduced somewhat in size from the normal bass and some players

15

Plate 4 VIOLIN FAMILY.
Left to right: violin, attributed
to Hans Krouchdaler, Oberbalm
(4519); viola, attributed to
Franz Straub, Friedenweiler
(4880); large viola by Ulrich
Reinhardt, Salzburg, 1672
(4522); violoncello, attributed
to Weiss, Basel or Krouchdaler
(4713); double bass, anonymous,
probably Brescian (2592). All
middle or second half of 17th
century and all in, or restored
to, original state.
(*Musikinstrumenten Museum,
Berlin*)

increased the number of strings so that the bass
strings were doubled an octave higher, as on
Mersenne's lirone. Other players added a set of metal
strings running below the ordinary strings. These
extra strings were not bowed; they sounded by
sympathetic vibration when the main strings were
bowed and they added a silvery shimmer to the
sound of the instrument. Such sympathetic strings
were to be used all over Europe later in the century
on the viola d'amore, which was originally a treble
viol with sympathetic strings, and on the baryton,
which, under the name of viol baritone, was a direct
descendant of the lyra viol, both of which retained
their popularity right through the eighteenth
century. Another small viol was the division viol or
viola bastarda. The English name derives from its use
in playing divisions and the Italian name from its
tuning, which was a mixture of fourths and fifths,
thus making it partly a viol and partly a violin and

hence a bastard. It remained a popular instrument
among virtuoso players into the eighteenth century.

The Violin

Violins were made in four, perhaps five, main sizes:
the treble, on the left of plate 4, which is the instrument known as the violin; the alto, the second and
third from the left, which is still the French name for
the viola and which is tuned a fifth lower so that the
lowest string is tuned to the C an octave below
middle C; occasionally a tenor, tuned a fifth or a
fourth lower still, about an octave below the violin,
and held between the knees like a small cello; a bass,
the violoncello, fourth from the left on the plate,
which is tuned an octave below the viola; and the
double bass, on the right of the plate, which is
tuned about an octave lower still. It is difficult to be
precise about the tuning of the double bass because
the number of strings, and thus the range, differed
from time to time and from place to place, according
to the ideas of the makers and the wishes of the
players.

Judging by the very small number that survive, the
tenor violin was the least often made of the family
and its use died out quickly, probably because
players found that they could cover its range equally
easily on the violoncello. The player's hand lies in a
natural position on the fingerboard of the cello,
whereas on the violin and the viola it is twisted
round to reach the fingerboard; the weight of the
cello is supported by the knees (the tailspike was not
adopted until the nineteenth century; before that
time cellists held the instrument gripped between the
knees), whereas the weight of a violin had to be
supported by the hand that was stopping the strings.
As a result it was far easier to play in high positions
on the cello than it was on the violin and solo works
for cello go much higher up the fingerboard than
those for violins did at this period, almost as high as
in modern works, and thus it was found that there
was no necessity for a separate tenor instrument.

The larger sizes of viola such as Andrea Amati and
Gasparo da Salò had made were still in common use,
and some other sizes of viola and cello were occasionally made during the later baroque period as we shall
see in due course. On the whole, however, the
standard instruments of the seventeenth century
were those that we know in our orchestras today,

but their sounds were different from those that we hear. The strings were all of gut and were at a lower tension than ours. The neck, and thus the string length, was shorter than it is today and the bridge was lower and less arched, so that the sound, although louder and brighter than that of the viol, was quieter and more gentle than that to which we are accustomed. Because the bow was quite differently shaped from the modern bow, with a long tapering point and either straight or curved slightly outwards, the attack was much more gentle at the beginning of a note.

The great violin makers of the first part of the seventeenth century were the Amatis. Of the two brothers Amati, who were the sons of Andrea Amati, himself one of the first great violin makers and the founder of the Cremonese school, Antonio had a fairly short career and sold out to his brother Hieronymus, also known as Girolamo, who was the better maker of the two. He in his turn was outshone by his son Nicola, the greatest of the Amati family, who was not only a superb maker but an outstanding teacher, his pupils including many of the greatest names of the next period. Da Salò and Maggini were still making violins in Brescia, which had earlier been far more important than Cremona as the main centre of violin making, but, as David Boyden relates, Galileo advised Monteverdi that the instruments from Cremona were much better than those from Brescia, an opinion reflected in the fact that even at that time, the first quarter of the seventeenth century, the Cremonese instruments were worth at least three times as much as those from Brescia.

Violin playing technique as well as manufacture was far more advanced in Italy than elsewhere, with Germany running a close second. The Italian bow grip was better suited to sonatas and other solo music than the French grip, which can be seen in plate II and which, with the shorter French bow, was better suited to dance music with its shorter bow strokes. The first composers to ask for different loudnesses were the Italians, Monteverdi, Fantini and Caccini, but Praetorius remarks of another instrument that it could get louder and softer like the violin, thus showing that this technique was known and practised in Germany early in the century. It is perhaps not surprising that the Germans followed

close upon the Italians when one remembers that many German composers, of whom Schütz is only one example, were trained and spent their early years working and writing in Italy and took home the Italian traditions established by the Italian composers.

An orchestra of violins had been formed in France by Louis XIII, the *Vingt-Quatre Violons du Roi* which consisted of six violins, twelve violas and six basses. Mersenne explains clearly that the violas were of three different sizes but that the strings of all three were tuned to the same four pitches; the three sizes were used to cover different parts of the range and for the sake of their different tone colours. He does not say whether all six basses were cellos or whether four, perhaps, were cellos and two double-basses; he does not mention the double-bass at all in this context. This string orchestra became famous all over Europe and it was envied and copied at other courts in other lands. The music it played was on the whole of a lighter nature than the Italian sonata and concerto, the new forms that were beginning to emerge, and it might almost be called a dance band. Mersenne's description of bowing technique makes it plain that the short bow, usually playing with single notes to a bow stroke, was the French style, as distinct from the longer bow and more legato bowing with several notes grouped in a stroke, which was already becoming characteristic of the Italian style.

The Continuo and Allied Instruments

Violins did not play alone, at least not in serious music, in Italy and Germany. They were always supported and their harmony amplified by the continuo. This is a blanket term covering one or more instruments playing the bass line of the music with at least one, and often several, instruments playing chords or arpeggios (broken chords played one note at a time, usually starting on the lowest note of the chord) based on that line and fitting the harmony of the music.

In the early seventeenth century there was a basic change in musical style. In the past composers had written polyphonic music, madrigals for example, with a number of strands of melody, each of equal importance, interwoven to form a network of music; now, however, there grew up a tradition of chordal music founded upon a bass line below a melody, between which a number of other instruments each played a note which was part of the appropriate chord. Vocal melody was accompanied in this way, growing from the recitatives of the early Italian opera; instrumental music of this sort derived from the dance, for which the tune was normally played by the highest instrument, supported by a simple chordal accompaniment. Sets of such dance tunes in four or five parts had been published by Susato and Attaignant and others from the middle of the sixteenth century and Praetorius published a set of over three hundred dances in 1612 under the title *Terpsichore*. During the early seventeenth century the style became more widespread and was not confined to the dance alone. There grew up a tendency for the highest and the lowest parts to be the most important, and the tenor, which had been so-called in the Middle Ages and the Renaissance because it held the melody, declined in importance and, with the alto, sometimes vanished altogether, leaving the top part supported only by the bass. This lowest part, both when it was the only accompanying part and when it was the lowest part of a group of players or orchestra, was called the continuo—perhaps because whatever else might stop the *basso continuo* continued—and was customarily played by several instruments simultaneously. String or wind instruments would play the bass line, and chordal continuo instruments (the keyboards such as harpsichord or organ, the bass lutes such as theorbo or chitarrone, and the harp) would play both the bass line and the appropriate chords or chordal figuration above it.

Initially the choice of these chords was left to the player, who was either the composer or who was expected to be sufficiently well-trained to be able to guess which chords were correct and which were coming next, and thus able to improvise a progression from one chord to the next which would make musical sense. This works well enough in simple music, but if there is any harmonic complexity it can cause difficulties, and so composers adopted the custom of adding numbers to the bass line, the figured bass, which told the player which chords to use. Interpreting the figures is simply a matter of counting up from the bass note, but it is necessary to know the conventions since a single figure can often imply a complete chord: no figure or a 3 indicates

a common chord in root position, eg, C E G C, the third, fifth and octave counting from the C at the bottom; a 6 indicates the same chord based on the third, the first inversion of the chord, eg, E G C, the third and the sixth counting from the E; and other figures indicate other chords. At most periods, in addition to these chords, the chordal continuo player was expected to improvise a melodic line which would both complement the line or lines that he was accompanying and lead smoothly and gracefully from one chord to the next; the clunk, pause, clunk of unrelated chords so often heard today are a modern aberration. Also a modern convention is the restriction of the chordal continuo to the harpsichord or organ; in the seventeenth and eighteenth centuries any convenient or suitable instrument was used and there are many pictures showing harps or bass lutes either by themselves or, more usually, playing with one or more keyboard instruments.

The Archlutes

Two types of bass lute were used for continuo purposes, both of which are shown in plate 5: the theorbo on the left and the chitarrone on the right, to use the names most commonly employed today to distinguish between them. In their own time there was a less rigid distinction, for both these names and the term archlute were used for both types of instrument. There was some geographical distinction, however, the longer instrument being known as the Roman theorbo and the shorter as the Paduan. A composer would seldom specify which one was to be used, for this would normally depend upon availability and upon the personal preferences of the player. Certainly the longer instrument with its greater string length for the open basses would have a better tone in the bass than the shorter instrument, but this might well be outweighed by its cumbersome size and by the fact that the shorter instrument often had a slightly larger body and thus a greater resonance. As the frontispiece shows, and there are many other illustrations from the two centuries covered by this book, the bass lutes remained popular as continuo instruments right up to the end of the eighteenth century. They were easily portable and could be used in or out of doors to provide the accompaniment for any fairly small group of players or singers. Despite the enormous revival of interest in the lute

Plate 5 ARCHLUTES. *Left:* theorbo by Matteo Sellas, Venice, 1637. Fitted for 7 double courses from each peg-box, though the basses are now strung singly; 12 ivory frets let into the fingerboard. (*Carel van Leeuwen Boomkamp Collection 71, Gemeente Museum, Den Haag*). *Right:* chitarrone by Magno Tieffenbrucker, Venice, 1608. 6 double courses on the fingerboard and 8 open basses from the upper peg-box. (*Donaldson Collection 26, Royal College of Music, London*)

at the present time, the archlutes have not yet been
used to any great extent, perhaps because fewer
archlutes than ordinary lutes have been made, and
perhaps also because not enough lutenists have
acquired the necessary skills in reading figured basses.
It should not be long, however, before they regain
their rightful place as the first choice among continuo instruments for domestic and chamber use.

The Lute

During this period lutes of ordinary shape also
acquired extra bass strings, which, even though they
ran over the fingerboard, were not usually fingered
but were treated as open basses like those of the
archlutes. The upper six courses were tuned, like
the strings of the viols, in fourths with a third in the
middle, and four or more bass courses were added.
These were the same lengths as the other strings but
were tuned down by steps, each course being a tone
or a semitone lower than the preceding; a course is
one or more strings, each tuned to the same pitch or
in octaves and sounded together as though they were
one string. Most of Dowland's music was written
for such a lute, one of which can be seen in plate 6,
as was much of the best lute music of the period,
which saw the final flowering of the instrument.
With its light and delicate body, so light that it almost
feels like thistledown when balanced on the hand,
and gut strings, the lute is an instrument of extreme
sensitivity, able to reflect every mood of its player
and its music. It can produce a strong, robust tone
and considerable volume in music that requires
it and yet remain so sensitive that it will murmur a
response to any word spoken in the same room.
Heavy instruments were made in the bad first period
of the lute's revival, but those days are happily over,
save with rare exceptions, and makers and players
have united with scholars and historians to recognise
that this lightness and sensitivity are the lute's chief
characteristics which give it its unique musical
qualities.

In the first part of the seventeenth century the lute
was still one of the preferred solo instruments and it
was regarded as the ideal instrument to accompany
the voice and to make one of a small chamber group.
Like the viols it did not suit the new styles of music
that came into fashion in the middle of the century
and, apart from occasional use by Bach and others, it

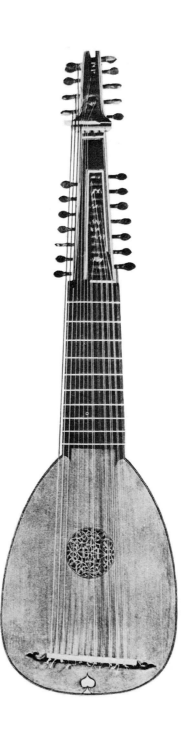
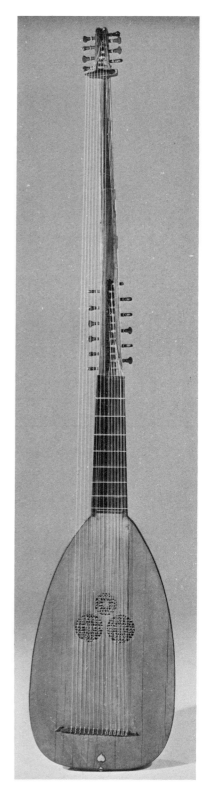

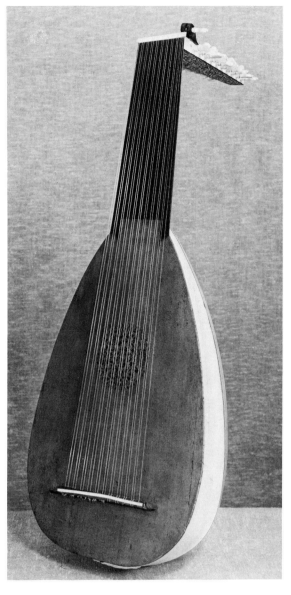

perature, or with the lapse of more than a few minutes between pieces, the strings will stretch, the body will swell or contract slightly, and the lute will go out of tune. Many observations about the time that it took to tune a lute, such as the oft-quoted slander that an eighty year old lutenist had spent sixty years tuning his instrument, are unkind exaggerations, but it is nevertheless undeniable that before a lute could be played it had always to be tuned, and thus any immediate desire to make music must always be temporarily frustrated.

A far more useful instrument for extempore playing, though with none of the lute's subtle beauties of tone colour or range of expression, was the cittern (plate 7), which in some respects can be thought of as the banjo of its period, the ideal instrument to take on an outing or for any impromptu singsong. Many engravings and woodcuts of this and the previous century show the cittern in use on such occasions and reveal its popularity for such casual music making, but it was also used for many more deliberate and serious occasions. The body was more strongly and solidly built than that of the lute, its flat back and tapering construction being more resistant to deformation through changes of temperature and humidity, and its wire strings held their tuning for days or more at a time.

As with the lute, there were also larger members of the cittern family. One of these was the ceterone, an instrument which resembled the chitarrone from the front but which had the flat back and tapering body of the cittern. There were also other large forms, each of individual shape and usually with a curvaceous outline which is known as festooned. The bandora or pandora appears in both Praetorius's and Mersenne's illustrations as well as surviving in a number of collections (plate 8); other patterns such as the orpharion (plate 91 in *The World of Medieval & Renaissance Musical Instruments*), the penorcon, the polyphant and the stump were less often seen. Indeed so confused and apparently interchangeable were some of these names that there is some controversy today about precisely what instrument each name implied. All had music especially written for them, but all could be regarded as lute substitutes for casual use, each substituting for a different size and tuning of lute. Donald Gill has recently provided a table of equivalents between lutes and citterns,

had vanished by the end of the century. Ironically enough, one of the major source books on the lute and its use, Thomas Mace's *Musick's Monument*, was published in 1676 as a despairing attempt to rescue the classic lute from the oblivion into which it was rapidly falling.

The Cittern

The lute, with a delicate and lightly built body and gut strings, has always suffered from the problems of stability. With any change of humidity or tem-

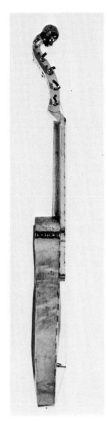

which is at least an attempt at sorting them out even though other scholars have already disagreed with it. All the larger sizes of cittern, like those of the lute, could be and were used as continuo instruments.

The Guitar

Even the guitar, an instrument which was becoming increasingly popular but which seems only rarely to have been made in larger versions, could be used as a continuo instrument for small groups, although its normal use was as a solo instrument and to accompany a singer as it still is today. It was known by various names, including gittern and quintern, the latter name probably because it had five courses, the uppermost single and the rest doubled like those of the lute. While a number of seventeenth century guitars had flat backs, as on the modern instrument (plates 9 and 10 right), others had slightly rounded backs like that on the left of plates 9 and 10, deepest opposite the bridge, though still with the vertical sides of the ordinary guitar. There were two varieties of guitar in the latter shape: the normal

Plate 9 GUITARS. *Left:*
chitarra battente by Giorgio
Sellas, Venice, 1627 (39). *Right:*
guitar by Antonio Stradivari,
Cremona, 1688 (41). Both with
5 double courses. (*Hill
Collection, Ashmolean Museum,
Oxford*)

Plate 10 GUITARS. Profiles
of the same instruments as in
plate 9, the Sellas on the left
and the Stradivari on the right.
(*Hill Collection, Ashmolean
Museum, Oxford*)

guitar with gut strings tied to the bridge in the normal manner, and the *chitarra battente* or plectrum guitar, which can be seen on the left of plates 9 and 10 and which, like the modern plectrum guitar, had metal strings that passed across the bridge and were fixed to the bottom of the body. The difference between these two instruments is thus entirely that of mechanical necessity; the bridge glued to the belly was strong enough to take the pull of the gut strings, but the greater tension of wire strings would have ripped it away, necessitating the greater security of pins driven into the bottom-block of the body. It is important to note that the same shape of body was used with both wire and gut strings and to recognise that the chitarra battente can be distinguished from the gut-strung instrument only by the continuation of the strings beyond the bridge and occasionally, but by no means invariably, by the fact that some chitarre battente have a broken belly, a change in the angle of the soundboard similar to that on the modern Neapolitan mandolin. It must be admitted that we do not yet really understand the distinction between the flat-backed and the rounded-backed gut-strung guitars, though it is tempting to think that it was mainly a matter of geographical preference and that some areas preferred the one form and some the other.

The Harp

An instrument more commonly used for continuo than the guitar was the harp. As in the previous period, a distinction was made between the single harp, a small instrument tuned only diatonically, with B flat and B natural as the only chromatic notes, as Mersenne shows on our plate 11, and the harp proper (plate 12), which by now was the triple harp, the instrument which was to become the national instrument of Wales, the only area where its use has never died out (see plate 62). As Mersenne points out in his text, the picture shows only the twenty-nine strings of the first rank, those nearest to the viewer, which are tuned diatonically from the uppermost tuning pegs, and the twenty-eight strings of the middle rank, which provide the chromatic notes and which are attached to the second row of tuning pegs. The third rank is not visible because, being furthest from the viewer, it is hidden by the others; it is tuned in unison with the first rank and its strings are attached to the lowest row of tuning pins and go to the furthest side of the table. A glance at plate 12 will show that Mersenne's artist has drawn the strings of the middle rank attached to the wrong pins, but the description in the text is quite clear. Mersenne goes on to point out that the harp has advantages over the lute, because every note is produced by the full length of a string, instead of many of them being played with the string stopped with the fingers, and over the harpsichord, because there are so many different ways of plucking the strings that a much greater delicacy and subtlety can be shown. Nevertheless, the greater ease and facility of playing via a keyboard, despite the greater portability of the other instruments, meant that the harpsichord and the organ were the most important of the continuo instruments.

The Harpsichord

Harpsichords existed in various sizes and with either one or two manuals. Italian instruments like that illustrated by Praetorius on our plate 22 were very commonly made with a single manual, and the instruments themselves were usually rather more lightly constructed than the Flemish harpsichords since they slid into a separate case for storage and transport. There were usually three choirs of strings, two at the normal pitch, which was known as 8′ from the length of the open organ pipe that sounded the bottom C of the keyboard, and one an octave higher at four-foot pitch. The soundboard carried two bridges, one for the 8′ strings and the other for the 4′, and these can be seen in Praetorius's picture. The strings are plucked by the jacks, which are hidden in the picture by the jack-rail, which prevents them from leaping out of the instrument. The jack is a slip of wood which stands on the inner end of each key. A slot is cut near the top of the jack to accept a tongue, which can swivel on a wire axle. A short piece of quill is fixed into a hole in the tongue, the best quills being those from a raven, crow or vulture, though some makers today are using a plastic such as Delrin instead. When the player depresses a key with his finger, the jack is pushed up past the string and, as it moves up, the quill comes against the string and plucks it, producing the sound. When the key is released the jack falls back and, as the quill touches the string, the tongue pivots on its axle, tipping the

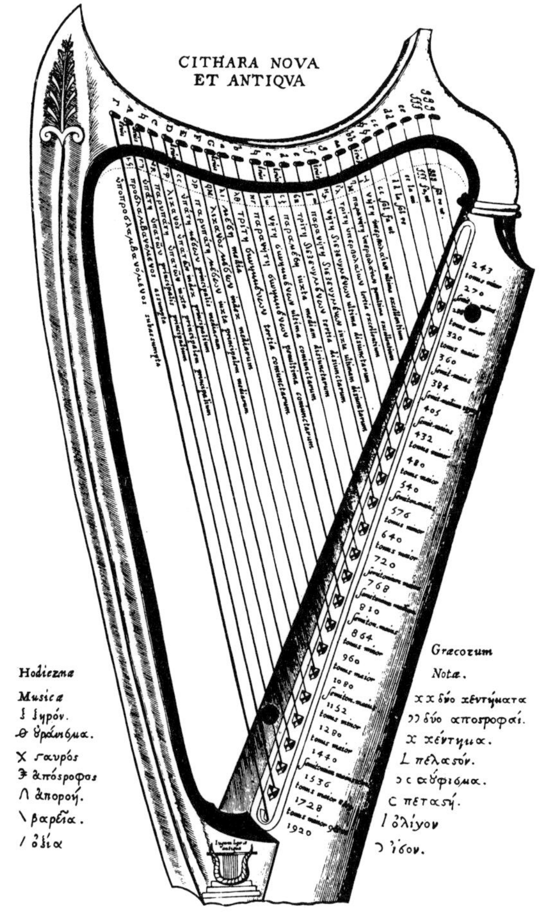

quill away from the string and preventing it from plucking the string for a second time. After the quill has passed the string, a spring, often a hog's bristle, pushes the tongue upright and the jack is ready to pluck again when required. A small piece of cloth fixed to the top of the jack acts as a damper and stops the sound of the string when the jack falls back. Each key has as many jacks as there are choirs of strings so that the player can use each choir by itself or can couple them all together.

One common feature of the keyboards up to the end of the seventeenth century was the use of the short octave at the bottom of the compass. Sharps and flats were seldom required in the extreme bass and the instruments were therefore built so that when the lowest key appeared to be an E, as it is in figure 1, it sounded a C and the other keys sounded the notes shown on them in the figure. If the lowest

Plate 11 Single harp, diatonic tuning with B flat and B natural. (*Mersenne*)

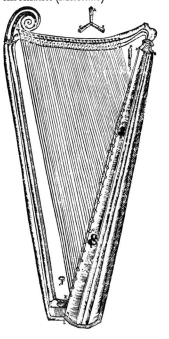

Plate 12 Triple harp, fully chromatic. (*Mersenne*)

Fig. 1 Keyboard bass short octave.

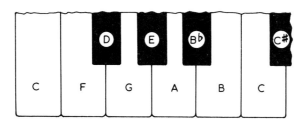

note appeared to be a B, as on some instruments with a larger compass, that key sounded the low G and the apparent C sharp sounded the A, and the D sharp the B, while the other keys produced their usual pitches. Only towards the end of the century were the low sharps and flats required and makers then provided for them by dividing the accidentals, with the back half raised slightly above the front half, so that the front half of the key produced the conventional short octave note and the back half played the normal accidental which one would expect from that key elsewhere in the compass. These split keys were not new, for instruments had been made in the earlier part of the century with some keys, usually the A flat and the E flat and sometimes one or two others, broken in this way. This was because, in the meantone tuning normally used at this period, a string tuned to A flat could not be used as a G sharp; if it were in tune for the one it would be badly out of tune for the other and would howl like a wolf against the notes being played with it. Even the least musical hearer would be much more conscious of these wolf notes on the organ than on the harpsichord because the sound of a plucked string dies away fairly quickly but the sound of an organ sustains at full volume for as long as the keys are held down, with the wolf howling all the time, and so such keys were very commonly provided on organs. Full details of the problems of meantone and other temperaments will be found in J. Murray Barbour's book and elsewhere, but briefly, the notes that were the worst affected were the G sharp/A flat, the E flat/D sharp, and then to a lesser extent, because they were less often used in both keys, the C sharp/D flat, the B flat/A sharp and the F sharp/G flat, giving in each case the most often used name of the note first. The G sharp/A flat was the note most often used under both names and therefore the one which was most often provided with a divided key. The virginals in plate 13 has the E flats and the A

flats divided, as well as the short octave. Mersenne, who as a mathematician was fascinated by tuning problems, illustrates organ keyboards with all the keys divided in this way and instruments with such keyboards have been built for theorists and others from the sixteenth century to the present day. All suffer from the same difficulties: each key must have its own strings or pipes, which makes them unwieldy and expensive, and the player has to remember which part of which key is supposed to be played with which other keys, so that these instruments are almost impossible to play in performance. As a result they have hardly ever been used by ordinary musicians and the most that one usually finds are the two or three most commonly divided keys such as those to be seen in plate 13.

There were two quite distinct varieties of double-manual harpsichord in the early seventeenth century. Some had two manuals, like all the later such instruments, as a means of obtaining varying tone qualities and volume, the so-called contrasting or expressive double; others had two manuals as a means of transposing, of playing in two different keys, for the two manuals were tuned a fourth or a fifth apart. The need for this facility, which was implicit in the way in which music had been conceived as being constructed from hexachords, as Nicolas Meeùs has pointed out, was already almost gone, for this concept of music hardly lasted into the seventeenth century, but nevertheless it was still sufficiently prevalent for the Ruckers dynasty of Antwerp, who were the most famous makers of harpsichords of their period, to build many instruments of this type. Plate III shows a harpsichord by Jan Ruckers, Hans the Younger, which is one of the only two known to survive as unaltered transposing double-manual instruments. The upper manual produces the sounds that one would expect from its keys; the lower manual transposes, so that when the F key is depressed, the jacks pluck the same strings as would the key above it on the upper manual and thus sounds a C. Plate IV shows a similar instrument built by Jan Couchet, the nephew of Jan Ruckers, built originally to the same pattern but converted at the beginning of the eighteenth century so that the keyboards are aligned with each other and produce different tone colours instead of different pitches.

Plate I 'Herzog August the Younger and his family', Albert Freyse, c. 1645. Six viols in consort with a singer. (*Landesmuseum, Braunschweig*)

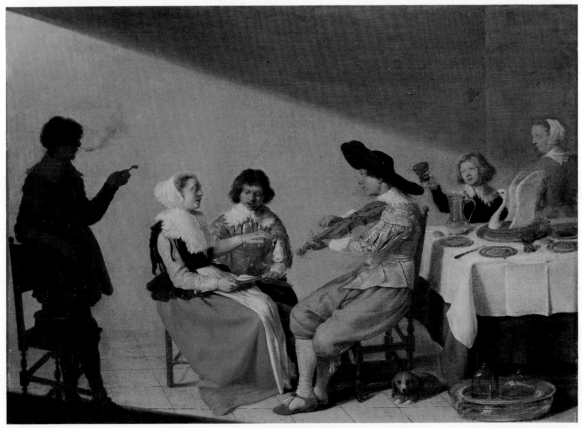

Plate II 'The Musical Party', Jacob van Velsen, before 1656. Violin held at the breast and played with a short French bow, accompanying singers. (*National Gallery, London, 2575*)

Plate III Transposing double-manual harpsichord by Jan Ruckers, Antwerp, 1638. C/E–c³, short octave in the bass, the apparent E sounding C, 1 × 8′, 1 × 4′ and harp. (*Russell Collection no. 6, Edinburgh University*)

Plate IV Contrasting double-manual harpsichord by Jan Couchet, Antwerp, 1646. GG/BB–c³, 2 × 8′, 1 × 4′. Originally transposing but converted early in the eighteenth century. (*Conservatoire Museum, Brussels, M.276*)

Plucking a string very close to one end, instead of two or three inches away from the end, will produce a different tone quality. So will touching the string with a small pad of leather near the end, and so will playing an 8′ and a 4′ string together instead of just an 8′ by itself. The transposing double could produce different tone qualities on either manual; it was possible to play on the 8′ strings alone, or with the 4′, and the buff leather could be slid across to touch the strings, but because both manuals used the same set of strings, the sound of one manual could not be contrasted with the other, nor could the selected sonority be changed until one stopped playing and altered the registration. Thus there were, in effect, two harpsichords built into the same box, one tuned a fifth higher than the other. Both used the same set of strings, with a buff batten to the 8′, but what appears to be a double-manual harpsichord is, musically speaking, two single-manual instruments. On the expressive or contrasting double, on the other hand, it was possible to play with one sonority on one manual and then change to the other manual with a different tone quality, for its jacks plucked a different set of strings. Indeed, the player could play on one manual with one hand, and on the second with the other hand, thus contrasting the tone quality of the two. The instruments were also constructed so that the two keyboards could be coupled together, allowing the player to play on all the strings simultaneously from one keyboard. The normal disposition on such instruments was to have a row of jacks for each rank of strings, and when there was an extra row of jacks it was usually placed to pluck one of the 8′ ranks at a different point on its length or equipped with plectra of different material, such as leather instead of quill, to produce a different tone quality.

The Virginals

As well as the full-size harpsichords, smaller instruments were built for domestic use, either in the rectangular shape such as that of the unusually large instrument in plate V, which was popular in Flanders and Britain, or in the polygonal shape to be seen in plate 13, which was more popular in Italy. Both types of virginals had a similar action, with the strings running nearly parallel with the front board and the row of jacks running diagonally across the

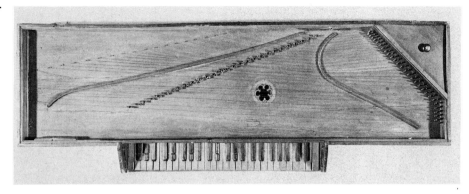

soundboard, so that although various names were used in their own day. and although in England the name of virginals was used for the harpsichord as well, the best names for them today are rectangular or polygonal virginals, according to their shape. Both work in exactly the same way as the harpsichord, though producing a somewhat different tone colour, but both have only one choir of strings, one set of jacks and one keyboard. The jacks are arranged in pairs, one plucking the string in front of the pair and the other the string behind.

The Clavichord

Another domestic instrument, much smaller and lighter than the virginals, although very small, easily portable virginals were made for ladies' boudoirs and for travellers, was the clavichord. This was a small instrument with less than half as many pairs of strings as there were keys on the keyboard, as can be seen in plate 14. This economy of size was achieved by taking advantage of the nature and mechanism of the instrument. On a harpsichord the string is plucked by the quill as it moves up past it, and the whole length of the string between the bridges is thrown into vibration and sounds the pitch demanded by its length and tension. On the clavichord, however, the string is made to vibrate by being touched by a tangent fixed to the end of the key, which rises and touches it hard enough to make it vibrate, and then remains in contact with it, so defining its length, for the sounding length of the string is that from the tangent to the bridge on the soundboard. Once the tangent drops away from the string the sound is stifled by the listing woven round its other end. Thus it is possible for more than one tangent to use each pair of strings, provided that

Plate 13 Polygonal virginals by Ionnes Battista Boni, Cortona, 1617. C/E-f³ with split keys for short octave and for D sharp/E flat and G sharp/A flat, 1 × 8′. (*Smithsonian Institution, Washington, 60.1392*)

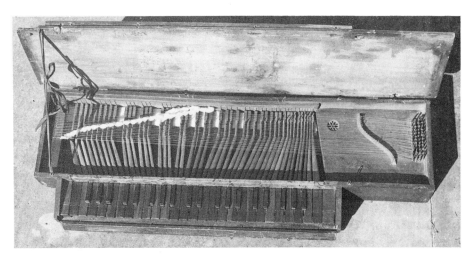

Plate 14 Fretted clavichord, anonymous, German, 17th century. C/E-c³. (*Dr. Rodger Mirrey*)

Plate 15 Positive or chamber organ, attributed to E. Hoffheimer, Vienna, 1592 or 1602. C/E-c³, flute 4′ and 2′, regal 8′ from B flat to c³, tremolo. Bellows pedal for the right foot. There is some confusion as to the origin of this instrument, due to the Viennese attribution, the inscription in Dutch over the doors, the inclusion of the arms of the Earl of Montrose in the decoration, and an alleged association with Princess Elizabeth, the Winter Queen. (*Carisbrooke Castle Museum, Isle of Wight*)

the distance from each tangent to the soundboard bridge is correct. To maintain the correct distance from the bridge, many of the key-levers of the fretted (*gebunden* in German) clavichord are cranked at varying angles. The tuning of the instrument is thus built into it by the maker and the player can alter it only slightly to suit his personal inclination and preference for one temperament or another, by bending tangents so that they are tipped over a little and stop the string nearer to, or further from, the bridge. On the other hand, he has the compensating advantage that he spends far less time tuning the clavichord than other keyboard instruments, since he needs to tune only four pairs of strings instead of twelve to each octave in most of the compass. A further advantage is that, because there are so few strings, there is much less strain on the casework and this can be light, reducing the weight of the instrument and increasing its resonance. The only musical disadvantage is that if two notes a tone or a semitone apart share a pair of strings, they cannot be played simultaneously because the only note that would be heard would be the one whose tangent was nearest to the bridge. As a result there are a few chords, such as dominant sevenths, that cannot be played, but this chord was not often used at this period. It was essential to be neat-fingered when playing trills in which both notes were sounded from the same pair of strings, but there has never been a period when neat fingering was a disadvantage and the dexterity acquired in this way was beneficial in the long run to a player's technique, even though it meant taking care at the time.

The Organ

The last of the continuo instruments to be considered is the organ. For domestic and theatrical performance this seems to have been quite a small instrument, a positive organ, such as that shown in plate 15, that could be moved from position to position with little more difficulty than a harpsichord. It is generally thought that Monteverdi's *organo di legno* was probably what later generations would call a box of whistles, a small organ with wooden flue stops, such as diapasons, and other flute stops. Only on larger organs built into churches and such buildings was it normal to find reed stops other than the regal, which is a reed stop normally without pipes but with small resonators, which took up little space and which can be seen in plate 15. Plate 16 shows a variety of flue pipes of different types to the left and regal and other reed pipes on the right, while plate 17 shows the reed itself in detail; anyone who has taken apart an old-fashioned bulb motor horn will recognise it immediately. The pitch of the reed is

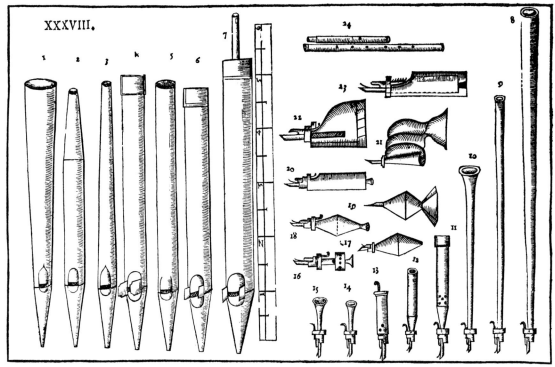

Plate 16   ORGAN PIPES.
Flue pipes on the left (the scale
only applies to these), reed
pipes and regals to the right;
a transverse flute above.
(*Praetorius*)

XXXVIII.

1. Dolcan. 4. Fuß.   2. Coppelfloit. 4. Fuß.   3. Flachfloit. 4. Fuß.   4. Klein Barduen. 8. Fuß.   5. Offenfloit. 4. Fuß   6. Gedact. 8. Fuß.   7. Rohrfloit: oder Holsfloit. 8. f.
8. Trommet. 9. Krumbhorn. 8. Fuß. 10. Schalmei. 8. 4. Fuß. 11. Sorduen. 16. Fuß. 12. Zinck : Cornet-Difcant. 13. Rancket : 8.16. Fuß. 14. Meffing Regahl. 8. Fuß
15. Gedempfft Regahl. 16. 17. 18. Krumbhorn. 19. 20. 21. 22. 23. Bart Pfeiffen allerley Art. 24. Querfloit.

controlled by the position of the wire bridle on its length, and the tone quality by the shape and the size of the resonator attached to it; various forms can be seen on the right-hand side of Praetorius's illustration on our plate 16. The size and complexity of organs varied considerably from one country to another, those of Germany, the Low Countries and France being more elaborate in the available tone colours than those of Britain and Italy. Even by the middle of the eighteenth century British organs lacked separate pedal pipes, the only use for pedals being to operate the lowest pipes on the manual by pull-downs such as can be seen on plate 59. By the beginning of the seventeenth century it was normal in most northern European countries to have full pedal sections with their own pipes.

An organ is a multiple instrument; the only single organs were the little portatives of the Middle Ages, which had entirely dropped out of use by this time. All others consist of a number of complete sets of pipes, which can be combined or alternated in order to produce different tone colours. The basic set of pipes speaks at the normal pitch for the key that controls them, and these are known as eight foot (8′) pipes because an open pipe that sounds the C two lines below the bass stave is eight feet long. A set which sounds an octave higher would be called four foot (4′) pipes, and those sounding an octave higher still are the two foot (2′) pipes. Those which sound an octave lower are called the sixteen foot (16′), and below that are the thirty-two foot (32′). Other lengths of pipe produce the fifth, the twelfth (an octave and a fifth), the tenth (an octave and a third) or other intervals above the pitch of the key depressed, and any or all of these pipes can be sounded together by drawing the appropriate stops. Because the tone quality of a pipe will depend on its shape, further sets of pipes of these lengths but of different shapes are added, so that by a judicious combination of pipes an almost infinite variety of tone quality and colour can be produced. The French, German and Dutch organs in particular had a greater range

29

Plate 17 Detail of organ
reeds with tuning bridles.
(*Mersenne*)

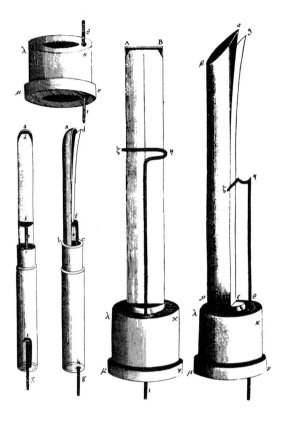

of tone colours available than those of other countries, and they were already tending towards the magnificent instruments for which J. S. Bach and his contemporaries composed, and in those areas there is little external difference between the organs of this period and those of the early eighteenth century.

Wind Instruments

Italian organs, like the English, were comparatively simple, but their church services depended less upon the organ for accompaniment. In churches such as St Mark's in Venice, choirs of instruments were used as well as choirs of voices; groups of sackbuts and cornetts in particular, but also woodwind and string instruments. It was found that the design of St Mark's, which had been constructed so that the strophe and antistrophe of early church music could be flung antiphonally to and fro from side to side of the basilica, was ideal for this style of music in which each instrumental and choral group could contrast with and answer the other. Indeed it is possible that

this style of music originated simply because the design of the building was ideal for it. The result was that other great churches were built after the same pattern, with a series of choir galleries down each side to accommodate the vocal and instrumental choirs. Of the instruments involved in such choirs, the majority of the woodwind and the string instruments were Italian, as they were over much of Europe, but the sackbuts, like the other brass instruments, seem to have come mostly from Germany, the brass makers of Nuremberg being unrivalled until the end of the century, and even thereafter still being acknowledged as the best makers of trumpets and trombones.

The Sackbut

The trombone (German, *Posaun*; English, *sackbut*) was the ideal instrument for accompanying the voice, for, with its slide, it could produce any note of the chromatic scale, and it was the only brass instrument with this ability for two centuries to come. In addition, it could play perfectly in tune and it is still the only brass instrument which is naturally able to do so. The long, comparatively funnel-shaped bell gave it sonority without the blaring sound of the modern instrument, which has a bell with a much sharper flare. The sackbut was made in a family of sizes, the most important of which was the ordinary or tenor instrument, which Praetorius numbers 3 on our plate 18, and if only one were in use with a choir it would normally be this size. The alto, number 4, and the bass, numbers 1 and 2, were also used, and sometimes the great bass (number 2 on plate 22 which is drawn to a different scale and can thus accommodate the larger instruments). Only in the treble was it weak, for the soprano trombone was the least successful size, and the cornett (German, *Zink*), an instrument that combined a trumpet-style mouthpiece with finger holes, was used for the upper parts.

The Cornett

Various sizes of cornett were used, the most important of which were the ordinary treble cornett, number 6 on plate 18, and the mute cornett or *stille Zink*, number 9 in Praetorius's illustration. The treble cornett was normally built on a curve by halving a piece of wood, hollowing it out and then re-uniting it with a sleeve of black leather over it to keep it airtight, and it was played with a miniature trumpet mouthpiece inserted into the end. The mute cornett was straight and made in one piece by being turned on a lathe; it had a small mouthpiece, more conical than that of the treble cornett and thus producing a much softer tone, turned into the wood of the top of the tube. A compromise instrument, with a tone somewhat between the two, was Praetorius's number 8, the straight cornett with a separate mouthpiece. All three were at the same pitch but each had its own characteristic tone quality. The larger and smaller cornetts shown on the same plate were less often used. The mute cornett was ideal for accompanying a single voice and the ordinary cornett was equally ideal for use with choirs or in chamber music. Its sound was delicate and soft and Mersenne says that the sound was ravishing when it was played well and that it was the ideal instrument for playing divisions, as variations and decorative figures in quick notes were called at that time (*diminutions* in French). He says that it can be played so gently that a song eighty *mesures* long could be played in one breath, and that there was one player who could, without difficulty, manage one hundred *mesures* in a breath.

This gentleness and extreme restraint, so important in the seventeenth century, seem to be the most difficult characteristics to achieve, for they are the least often heard in modern revivals. However, as techniques improve, and even in the last decade there has been a noticeable difference, we may hope that this technique will be rediscovered. The cornett has suffered, more than most instruments in the modern early music revival, from the lack of opportunity for players to specialise on an early instrument. The majority of modern cornettists are also professional trumpeters and it is not possible successfully both to earn a living on the trumpet and to play the cornett occasionally, for the mouthpieces are very different, that of the cornett being about half the size of that of the trumpet and with a much narrower rim. The result has been that players have had mouthpieces specially made to fit into the cornett but which retain the rim and cup of their normal trumpet mouthpieces, with disastrous effects upon their cornett tone. Only recently have some of the better players come to realise that such com-

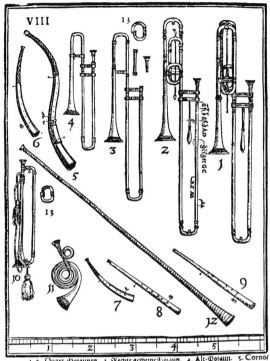

Plate 18 BRASS INSTRUMENTS. Sackbuts and cornetts above, cornetts and coiled and folded trumpets below, alphorn diagonally. The tenor trombone (3) and folded trumpet (10) are each shown with a whole-tone crook (13). (*Praetorius*)

promises cannot be successful and to recognise that what such leading players and makers as Christopher Monk have been saying for many years is true: that only the proper mouthpiece, the size and shape of the cup of an acorn, can produce the proper sound.

The Trumpet

The same thing is true of the trumpet, and players who once scoffed at the early trumpet mouthpieces that Eric Halfpenny described in detail in the *Galpin Society Journal*, saying that they could not be typical or that they were military mouthpieces, have come to realise that only with this type of mouthpiece, huge as a bucket as it seems to our modern eyes, is it possible to obtain the range required in this and the succeeding period with the facility, the quietness and the tone quality that the music demands.

The trumpet shows comparatively little change from the Renaissance instrument, as may be seen by comparing plate 19 with plate 76 in *The World of Medieval & Renaissance Musical Instruments*, the bell

Plate 19 Trumpet by Augustine Dudley, London, 1666. Brass with silver mounts. (*Museum of London*)

flare still being more gradual than on the instruments of the High Baroque, but the range that the instrument was expected to cover was growing rapidly. Whereas in Monteverdi's *L'Orfeo* the highest note is G, the twelfth harmonic (see Figure 2 on page 56), with a single A, the tone above, as a passing note, the music in Fantini's trumpet tutor, published only thirty years after *L'Orfeo*, goes up to top C and makes much more use of the upper part of the range. Monteverdi was writing an extended and elaborate fanfare, but Fantini was writing sonatas for the trumpet as a fully melodic solo instrument, a considerable change of use, which was to be extended a great deal further in the next period.

The Timpani

We know little of the appearance of the timpani at this period. Few surviving pairs are datable with any accuracy and one of the best sources is Praetorius's illustration shown in plate 20, which includes a military side drum. Unlike the trumpet, there is little surviving music for the timpani and we have to rely on written descriptions, and illustrations of them in use in processions when the drums themselves are usually hidden by banners, to tell us that they were used as the normal bass for the trumpets, improvising their parts from those of the trumpeters.

The Woodwind

Here also there was little change from those of the late Renaissance. Bob Marvin's research into recorders indicates that slight changes to bore shape were made in order to alter the tuning for, as chordal playing became more important and the meantone temperament came to be adopted, various intervals had to be changed. The dissonant Pythagorean thirds, in particular, became rather flatter in order to be better in tune harmonically. There is some evidence to suggest that larger instruments were made in the seventeenth century than had been usual in the sixteenth, though because only a few such instruments have survived and because there is nothing comparable with Praetorius's *Syntagma Musicum* for the sixteenth century it is difficult to be sure just when these larger instruments came into use. Thus, when we look at plate 21, which shows shawms of the sizes that were familiar in the Renaissance, and at plate 18, which shows the normal sizes of sackbuts, and at plate 2, which shows the ordinary sizes of viols, and then look at plate 22, which shows larger sizes of all these instruments, we wonder whether these were new in Praetorius's period or whether they had been used previously. Bass trombones a fourth lower than the tenor (plate 18, numbers 1 and 2) certainly existed in the sixteenth century, but were true bass trombones (plate 22, number 2), an octave below the tenor, in use before 1600? Equally, we are sure that bass shawms (plate 21, number 1) already existed, but the great contrabass shawm, over three metres long and far taller than its player (plate 22, number 3—note the scale on the plate) seems to have been new.

There are a number of other woodwind instruments illustrated by Praetorius of which we know nothing at all since examples do not survive. There are, for example, some instruments described in Julius Schlosser's great catalogue of the Vienna Kunsthistorisches Museum collection as *Sordunen*, but they bear little or no resemblance to the instruments that Praetorius illustrates under that name. Also illustrated by Schlosser is what purports to be a *bassanello* (Catalogue no. C.218), but this is quite obviously the body of a Renaissance bass flute as Eric Halfpenny pointed out in *Galpin Society Journal XIII*. There are no bassanelli, Sordunen or Schryari known to survive and the only hope is that some

1. Heerpaucken. 2. Goldaten Trummeln. 3. Schweizer Pfeifflin 4. Amboß

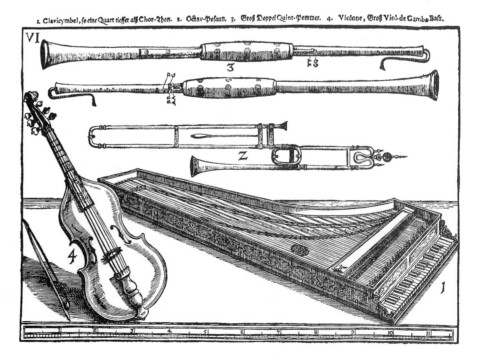

1. Bas-Pommer 2. Baßet oder Tenor-Pommer. 3. Alt Pommer.
4. Discant Schalmey. 5. KleinSchalmey. 6. Grosser Bock.
7. Schaper Pfeiff. 8. Hümmelchen. 9. Dudey.

1. Clavicymbel, so eine Quart tieffer alß Chor-Thon. 2. Octav-Posaun. 3. Groß Doppel Quint-Pommer. 4. Violone, Groß Viol-de-Gamba.Baß.

Plate 20 DRUMS. Timpani above, side drums below, anvil and hammers bottom right, timpani tuning key and fifes in the centre. (*Praetorius*)

Plate 21 Shawms and pommers above and to the right, bagpipes to the left. (*Praetorius*)

Plate 22 LARGE INSTRUMENTS. *Top to bottom:* great bass shawm, back and front; great bass sackbut; great bass viol or violone; Italian harpsichord, C/E-c^3 , 2 × 8′ & 1 × 4′, inner and outer case. (*Praetorius*)

may one day turn up, perhaps in museums in Italy, which are still but little known, or in private collections there or in Spain or Austria, all places in which such finds have been made in the past. It is about these instruments in particular that Praetorius is so valuable, for his is the only guide to their appearance and this, combined with his descriptions of their range and their use, has allowed modern makers to produce conjectural reconstructions of these instruments. Several have proved to be very useful for the performance of late sixteenth and early seventeenth century music, but there is a tendency to forget that they are, as yet, conjectural and to assign altogether too much validity to them.

Transverse flutes, which were still mainly military instruments, recorders, shawms and curtals continued to be used from the end of the Renaissance and were still often used in families. These changed little in shape and appearance during the first half of the seventeenth century, save that most became more slender, being made with rather thinner walls. One surviving curtal, of uncertain date but probably

from the middle of the century, serves as an augury of things to come. This instrument, which can be seen in plate 23, is in transition from the curtal to the bassoon, for although it is still a curtal it is made in separate joints like the bassoon. The old curtals had been made from one piece of wood with two parallel tubes down it, joined by a short horizontal bore at the bottom of the instrument, as can be seen in plate 75 of *The World of Medieval & Renaissance Musical Instruments*. Now the double tube section has shrunk to the lower part of the instrument, and set into it is a narrow section, forerunner of the bassoon's wing joint, and a wider section, which will become the long joint of the bassoon. Only the added bell, which carries the bassoon down to the low B flat from the curtal's lowest note of C, is lacking, and that will be added during the next generation.

There were many less important instruments throughout the periods which are covered by this book, many of them instruments which were only occasionally used. Some were played by travelling virtuosi, of whom there seems to have been an almost inexhaustible supply, players who were, for a while, the talk of the town and who then moved on to other centres where they might again reap the rewards of the novelty of the instruments they played or the way in which they played them; Mozart, as a child and again as a young man, was one of these wandering minstrels in the latter part of the next century. Pepys is one of those who mentions a number of such performers; he was himself an enthusiastic musician and observer of instruments, ever ready to hear and often to try a new instrument and his information is often valuable. For instance, his oft-quoted description of the Great Fire of London, with boats fleeing across the River Thames, many of them with a virginals among their baggage, is an indication of the extent to which households possessed such instruments and included people who wished to play on them, or perhaps, to seek a parallel closer to our own times, wished merely to impress the neighbours by having one in the parlour, surmounted by whatever was the seventeenth century equivalent of the aspidistra.

One of the many instruments that Pepys went to hear played was the tromba marina (plate 24), an instrument usually built with only one string. The string was not stopped in the normal way but was touched lightly with a finger to persuade it to break into its aliquot parts and sound the various overtones of the harmonic series. Thus it played the same notes as the natural trumpet, which explains why it was called a tromba; there are several theories, none of which is convincing, about the marina part of the name, and rather than quote any of them it is more honest to say that we have not the slightest idea of how the name arose. The resemblance to the sound of a trumpet was enhanced by the design of the bridge, which has two feet of unequal size and weight. The string rests immediately above one foot, which is much thicker than the other; the lighter foot is fractionally shorter than the other so that it rests only lightly on the belly of the instrument. As the string vibrates, this lighter foot buzzes against the soundboard or against a plate of bone or ivory let into the soundboard and, when all is properly adjusted, which takes a little care and trouble, the sound is remarkably like that of the trumpet. Although not all these instruments were so equipped, the instrument being played in plate 24 has a number of sympathetic strings inside the box, which would help to amplify the sound and add a ringing tone to its quality. As can be seen in the photograph, the instrument was bowed with the bow above the stopping hand. This was presumably so that the hand would not be inhibited from finding the correct harmonic positions on the string, especially those halfway and one-third of the way along the string, essential for the second and third harmonics, which might otherwise be near to the bowing point.

An added interest of this picture is that the player is Canon Galpin. It was he who established the first important modern collection of early instruments in Britain, a collection most of which is now the Leslie Lindsey Mason Collection of the Museum of Fine Arts, Boston, and which once included a number of other instruments illustrated in this book (eg plates 33 and 36). He was one of the first to study the older musical instruments and he emphasised the attitudes which have been characteristic of the Galpin Society, which was founded by his friends and named in his memory: that it is only by studying and playing old instruments that we can understand the intentions of composers of earlier times, and that music

Plate 23 Bass curtal (*Choristfagott*) made in three joints. Probably Italian, mid-17th century. (*Kunsthistorisches Museum, Wien, C.201*)

Plate 24 Tromba marina, Italy, second half 17th century, played by Canon Francis W. Galpin, prior to 1910. The instrument is now in the Museum of Fine Arts, Boston, no. 17.1733. (*F. W. Galpin, Old English Instruments of Music, London, 1910*)

often sounds best when it is played on the instruments for which it was written, thus stressing the importance of actually playing such old instruments as survive in playable condition, as the Canon was doing when the photograph was taken.

One last indication of changing tastes and ideas should be noticed. Whereas Praetorius's book published in 1619 is an outstanding achievement in a series of musical encyclopedias, a series which began with Virdung in 1511 and continues into our own time, Mersenne's book, published in 1636, is a new phenomenon, for it is primarily a scientific treatise and only incidentally an encyclopedia of musical instruments. Proportional figures can be seen on many of his illustrations and much of his text is devoted to the analysis of sound and of harmonies.

Such scientific interest, which can be seen as a reversion to the approach of the medieval schoolmen and classical philosophers, who regarded music as a branch of mathematics, becomes increasingly important to the history of musical instruments and this is perhaps the beginning of the battles between the acousticians, who know how an instrument *should* be made in order to produce the best sound, and the instrument maker who, in serving his apprenticeship, has garnered the wisdom of his ancestors and thus knows how it *is* made. The unfortunate musician stands between these opponents, veering now one way and now the other, concerned only to have an instrument that will allow him to play the music he wishes to play, with the least effort and to the best effect, producing the most beautiful sound and the fewest wrong notes.

Chapter II
The High Baroque

The period of the High Baroque is, musically speaking, a climax that has never been surpassed, though this is something that can be said of almost any period depending upon the taste of the writer. Different authors have used different names for this period, so let us resort to personalities and describe it as the period from the birth of Corelli in 1653, a purely arbitrary date, to the death of J. S. Bach in 1750, which was indeed the end of an epoch even though, for music has no watertight compartments, the new style which followed was already by then well under way.

It was the age of the composer who was also a virtuoso. Violinists, such as Tartini, Vivaldi and Corelli, Marais, who was responsible for the final flowering of the viola da gamba, Couperin, Scarlatti, Handel and Bach, to name only a few of the great keyboard players, all astounded the world by their own playing as well as by the music that they composed. Much of the music of this period is lost to us, for all these composers were famed throughout Europe for the quality of their improvisations, music composed on the spur of the moment and performed at the instant of composition, never to be heard again. Even the music that was written down and published is but a pale shadow of what was heard by contemporary audiences, as we shall see in the course of this chapter. And this is the period in which we first have audiences, at least for instrumental music, for this is the period in which public concerts began. No longer is music confined to the theatre, to the church and to the palaces and chapels of the powerful and the wealthy. In Britain, Thomas Britton, the musical small-coal man as he was known to his contemporaries, for he was a coal seller by trade, began his public concerts, which were among the first in Europe and an example that was followed elsewhere as clubs and collegia gradually opened their doors to all comers and became public concerts. Not that this reduced the demand for music by the nobility and by those wealthy enough to patronise and employ artists themselves, for the princely and episcopal courts were still the most important patrons of composers and their main financial support. Throughout the seventeenth and eighteenth centuries and into the nineteenth century, the composer's hopes rested on the purse full of gold which acknowledged a fulsome dedication, just as many musicians' livelihoods depended upon the security of a position in a nobleman's private orchestra.

Public concerts, small as they were to begin with, often held in small rooms, did open the door to an appreciation of music by the public as a whole, and they led to the great concerts of instrumental and choral music that encouraged composers from Handel onwards to write their oratorios and other major works. At the same time, the acceptance of such works in the secular world encouraged the expansion of the forces used for church music, so that composers such as Bach were able to use far larger instrumental combinations in their cantatas, masses and passions than had been possible for the generation of composers before them, such as Schütz and Buxtehude. This was in part a result of increase in trade, which meant that there was more money available for spending in this way, especially in the great mercantile centres, but it was also the result of great and sweeping changes in musical instruments which led to the creation of new instruments which were suitable for such performances.

What led to this initially was a king's vanity. Louis XIV, who enjoyed the thought of himself as a dancer and who joined in the court ballets, could not bear that such performances could take place only out of doors in the fine weather of summer with the old loud instruments, the shawms and the sackbuts, as accompaniment. He wanted such music indoors as well. Only violins, with the addition perhaps of recorders, could play indoors without deafening the court and, if a greater range of wind sonorities was required, a range of new instruments was needed to provide them. Thus it was the wind instruments, particularly the woodwind, that went through the greatest change in this period. Instruments that had been adequate for outdoor music, for dance music and for festivities in large buildings, simply could not blend into an orchestra with string instruments, and it is noticeable that the composers of the early seventeenth century did not try to make them do so. A small recorder might be used as a bright splash of colour on the top of a string band; sackbuts and cornetts would be used with voices and perhaps to contrast with a group of strings playing with other voices; recorders would play as a group by themselves, but reed instruments could not be used with any other instruments save for brass and percussion and certainly not with strings. Now with the popularity of the *ballets du cour*, of the opera, with the desire for indoor music either with mixed bands of wind and string or at least for the wind players to be indoors without deafening the audience, intruments had to be modified so that they could be used in these new roles. More important, perhaps, music was becoming more complex, as it does in every new generation, and composers were writing parts with a wider range to such an extent that the older instruments could not cope with them.

The Talbot Manuscript

There are in this period no encyclopedic sources comparable with Praetorius and Mersenne and we are left, just at this time when all instruments changed from those of the High Renaissance and Early Baroque into those of the High Baroque, from those known to Lawes and Schütz to those used by Purcell, Bach and Handel, with no other information than what can be gleaned from examining the instruments which chance has preserved for us. In surveying these we should never forget the caveat expressed by Eric Halfpenny, that only the bad instruments survive— the good ones are used and patched and repaired until finally they fall apart. Fortunately this is not entirely true, for by accident the occasional good instrument may survive, but only too often it is the elaborate and ornate instruments built, so far as one can see, solely to satisfy the noble and wealthy collector's desire for conspicuous consumption, with eye-catching beauty and the tone quality of a lump of pig-iron, which survive in quantity, while far fewer ordinary instruments are preserved. Of those

which do survive, many a plain and utilitarian instrument shows the modifications of one style of music, of one desired sonority, upon another, as the professional player endeavours to retain an instrument now out of style and out of date but yet beloved for its willing response and mellow sound.

One descriptive source survives and so far no other has been found. This is James Talbot's manuscript, dating from between 1685 and 1701 and preserved in the Christ Church Library, Oxford, much of which has been published section by section in various volumes of the *Galpin Society Journal*. The manuscript does not cover all instruments; if Talbot had any idea of publishing a treatise such as that of Mersenne, it was an intention never to come to fruition. Some instruments are described and measured in detail; others, including, as is so often the case, those of which we know the least from other sources, are merely mentioned by name with little or no information. Where measurements are given, they are often exact to the millimetre, for Talbot measured in feet, inches, eighths of an inch and halves or thirds of an eighth. Like Mersenne he consulted the leading professional musicians of his day and he borrowed instruments from them to examine and measure, usually those of the finest makers such as Bressan and Bull. His information fills many gaps in our knowledge, including the range of instruments produced by certain makers, what instruments were in use in England at that period, and on some instruments which have failed to survive, his is the only information that we have.

Woodwind Instruments

The Musette

Curiously, it was the French court's fascination with the simple life, with a bogus rusticity, that provided much of the technological know-how for the change to a greater complexity. The bagpipes such as those on plate 21 were peasants' instruments, and would thus be inappropriate for the mock-peasants of the court, for it was not suitable for royalty and the courtiers to play on an ordinary peasant's bagpipe with its roaring drones, nor to puff out their cheeks and exhaust themselves like a genuine sweaty peasant. Makers, especially the Hotteterre family and their associates, devised a new variety of bagpipe, the *musette du cour* (plate VI). This was a far more complex instrument than the older seventeenth century musette. It had a double chanter carrying a number of keys added to the shuttle drone, which was a cylindrical block of wood or of ivory in which a number of bores had been drilled so that the drone note could be altered to suit music in different keys by moving the shuttles, which were sliders that controlled which drone bore was to sound. The musette was blown by bellows strapped to the player's waist and operated by the elbow so that he could, if he wished, sing to his own accompaniment, for another alteration made for the court was to quieten the instrument to make it better suited to polite society. This form of bagpipe was the direct ancestor of the Northumbrian small pipes and of some other parlour bagpipes of our own times.

The experience that wood-turners gained in turning the musette's delicate external patterns and narrow, accurately profiled bores, was applied to other woodwind instruments. The pipes of the musette each ended in a tenon which was set into a stock, the block which is tied into the mouth of the bag, and makers realised that other instruments could also be made in short pieces called joints, linked together with sockets and tenons. Shorter joints made it easier to control the bore profile because shorter reamers could be used, allowing far greater control and accuracy of shaping, for however carefully it is done, there is bound to be some whip or chatter of the tool when a tube that is the full length of a flute or shawm is reamed. Another advantage of the short joints was that makers were able to ream different parts of the bore differently and so make it easier for the player to obtain a wider range and also to get various notes better in tune. No instrument is naturally perfect and only by 'cooking the bore', by cheating and deliberately avoiding a theoretically pure bore, is it possible to get all or most of the notes in tune. Deliberate inaccuracy in the right places makes an almost perfect instrument!

The Recorder

The result of all this was that instruments were made in three or more pieces with sockets and tenons to fit into each other. The recorder was made in three pieces as can be seen on the right hand side of plate 25; a head, which included the mouth of the instru-

ment and which was more or less cylindrical in bore, ending in a socket; a body, which was conical in bore with the widest part at the head end, with six finger holes and a thumb hole, and with a tenon at the top and at the bottom; and a foot, which was also conical but rather more sharply so than the body, with one finger hole for the little finger and a socket at the upper end. Because the foot was on a separate movable joint, only one little-finger hole was needed, for it could be turned to suit the little finger of either the left or the right hand, whichever the player preferred to have below the other, and thus the old French name of *flûte à neuf trous* gave way to a new name of *flûte à bec*.

When, in the early eighteenth century, Bach, Handel and their contemporaries called for the flute in their music, it was the recorder that they meant by this name. The recorder was still the respectable flute, the flute that was used for serious music, and the instrument that we call the flute today was only just beginning its rise towards respectability from being the common people's and the soldier's instrument. Its rise in the middle of the eighteenth century was aided by the fact that it was played by the Prussian Emperor, Frederick the Great, and by the fact that it was capable of greater expression and flexibility than the recorder. Nevertheless, it was still new enough as an instrument for serious music that it was always described by its mode of performance, *flauto traverso*, or cross flute in English, or as the *flûte d'Allemagne*, German flute. Flute without other qualification in any language always meant the recorder up until about 1750.

The end of the seventeenth and the first half of the eighteenth centuries was the period of the greatest recorder makers: in London Bressan (plates 25 and 26) and the two Stanesbys, father and son; in Brussels the Rottenburgh family; in Amsterdam Haka; in Nuremberg the two Denners; in Paris the Hotteterre family and their colleagues. The instruments of all these makers are of supreme quality in both sound and appearance, some with massive ivory mounts and ferrules, others of plain wood, but all of such superb design, that they are the basis and the models of today's reconstructions, whether made of wood or of plastic.

The recorder was still made in a family of sizes, the most important of which, *the* recorder unless

Plate 25 Two voice flutes by Peter I. Bressan, London, *c.* 1700, one disjointed to show the parts. One showing the finger holes, the other the thumb hole. (*Frans Brüggen*)

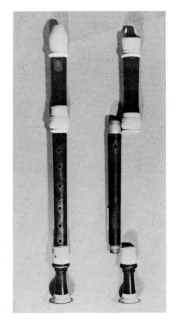

Plate 26 RECORDERS.
Right to left: treble (alto), voice
flute, tenor, bass with its strut
between it and the tenor. The
mouthpipe on the bass is
modern. All by Peter I. Bressan,
c. 1700. (*Grosvenor Museum,
Chester, 507.L.25*)

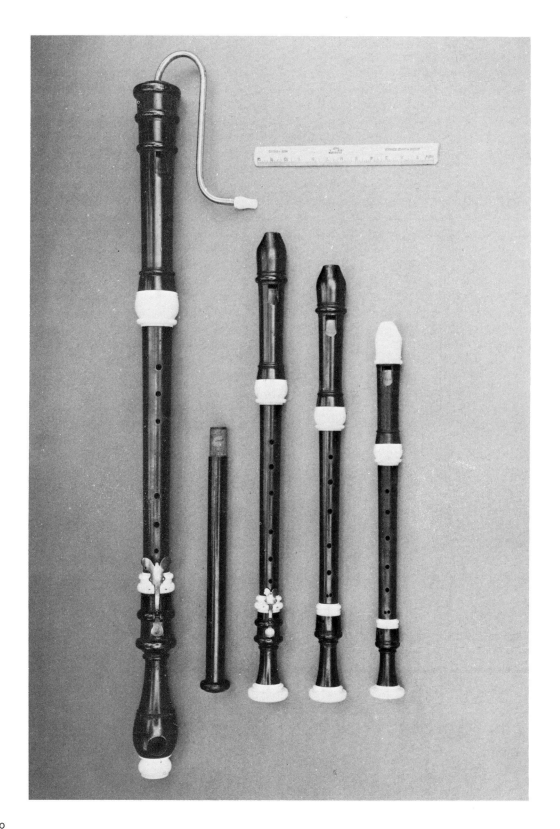

otherwise specified, was the treble (also often called the alto today), the smallest in plate 26, whose lowest note is the F above middle C. As in today's reconstructions, other sizes were the descant or soprano (lowest note C) above the treble, and below it the tenor, with the lowest note middle C, the largest but one in plate 26, and the bass, with F as the lowest note, the largest in the plate. The great number of surviving basses by these and other makers suggests that they may have been more commonly used in the late seventeenth and early eighteenth centuries than they are today. Bressan strengthened their tone, which tends to be weak, by providing a peg, or strut as Eric Halfpenny named it, which can be seen in plate 26. This was a hollow rod, the air column within which resonated in sympathy with the notes produced by the instrument and helped to strengthen them when it was inserted into the lower end of the instrument; in addition, since the end of the strut rests on the floor, some vibration is carried by it to the floor, which will itself resonate to some extent. A hole in the side of the bell fixes the acoustical length of the air column and acts as the open end of the instrument.

As well as the F and C series of recorders, a D and A set was commonly used, at least in England; known as voice flutes (plate 25 and the second in plate 26), they were pitched a minor third lower than the normal set. Their use seems to have died out sooner than that of the F and C set, for most of those that survive appear to have been made quite early in the eighteenth century. Very small instruments were also used, usually referred to as a piccolo or *flauto piccolo;* the concertos by Vivaldi for piccolo were for a small recorder, not for a small transverse flute as the name would imply today, and this usage lasted almost to the end of the eighteenth century for it is thought that Mozart's piccolo parts were played on either a small recorder or a flageolet. Much more problematic are the *flauti d'echo,* which Bach specified for the fourth *Brandenburg Concerto.* The music, with a considerable number of accidental sharps, looks more suited to an instrument in G than to the normal treble in F, but the presence of occasional low Fs and F sharps in the second recorder part makes such a hypothesis untenable, and, apart from the normal assumption that they are likely to have been a recorder of some kind, we have to say that we have

no idea of what they were, a frustrating position to be in with music that is so well known and so frequently played.

The Flageolet

The recorder was popular as the instrument for the professional musician and for the good amateur. A simpler version existed for the less competent amateur, and this was the flageolet. There is a basic distinction between the two instruments of that name, the serious amateur's instrument, which was also used by professionals and a developed form of which was used for the quadrilles in Jullien's concerts at the Crystal Palace in the latter part of the nineteenth century, and the simple amateur's instrument. The former instrument is the French flageolet, which had four finger holes and two thumb holes, and the front and the back of which can be seen in the middle and on the right of plate 27. The simpler instrument is the English flageolet (to the left of the plate), which has only half a dozen finger holes and no thumb holes. It was often made of wood or ivory to look like a small recorder; later versions made of metal or plastic were called the tin whistle or penny whistle. The English flageolet became a more elaborate instrument in the nineteenth century, but in the eighteenth century it was, as a simple pipe, an easy equivalent to the recorder and adequate for domestic and informal performances of music that was not too difficult to play.

One other use for both types of flageolet was in teaching caged birds to sing, which seems to have been so popular a pastime in the early eighteenth century that specially small flageolets were made for this purpose, as well as other instruments such as miniature barrel organs for those who found it easier to turn a handle than to play the same tune over and over until the birds had learned it.

The Transverse Flute

We may conclude that the cross flute was beginning its rise towards respectability from the fact that it comes first in the title of Jacques Hotteterre's manual, *Principes de la Flute Traversiere ou flute d'Allemagne, de la Flute à Bec ou flute douce, et du Haut-Bois,* and from the frontispiece of that work, which shows a well-dressed gentleman playing the instrument. One of a number of other such pictures

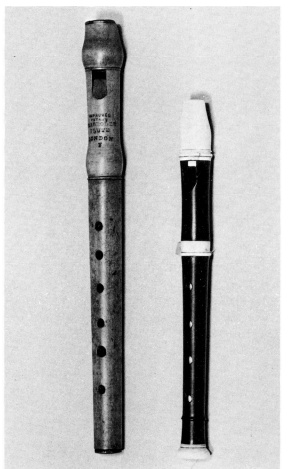

Plate 27 FLAGEOLETS. *Left to right:* English flageolet, anonymous (*Author's Collection, IV 64*); French flageolet, anonymous (*Carse Collection, Horniman Museum, London, 14.5.47/276*), showing the finger holes; the same French flageolet showing the thumb holes.

required, save by the avant-garde composers of the day.

Despite its name, it was almost certainly in France that the new form of the instrument was created, probably by one or more of the Hotteterres. This family of players and instrument makers at the French court is normally credited with the invention of the new model of the transverse flute, but the instruments that have come down to us, such as that illustrated on plate 28, simply bear the mark Hotteterre and it has, so far, proved impossible to determine which member of the family, which included at least four makers, was responsible for what instruments, nor do we know to which of them we should assign the credit for the instrument's invention. Like the recorder, the German flute was made in three separate joints: the head with the embouchure, the hole across which the player blows; the body with six finger holes, and the foot, a short joint, which carried a single key. Again like the recorder, the body was conical in bore, widest at the end nearest to the embouchure and gradually narrowing towards the foot, with a brief expansion of the bore from the key-hole to the end. The transverse flute has fewer finger holes than the recorder, only six instead of eight. There is no need for a thumb hole, which helps the recorder player to overblow into the upper octave, for the traverso player can achieve this by slightly altering the angle at which he blows across the embouchure and by increasing the speed of the air stream from his mouth. The little-finger hole on the recorder is an extension that on the tenor recorder (which is the same size as the transverse flute) takes the range down to middle C; the lowest note on the traverso was D and thus that hole was not needed.

The key on the foot joint was the first chromatic key to be fitted to a flute of either variety. Open-standing keys had been used on the larger recorders to cover holes which, on the smaller instruments, had been covered by the fingers but which were beyond their reach on the larger sizes. The key of the remodelled transverse flute had quite a different function: it was sprung so that it stood closed and it covered a hole between the open end of the instrument and the first finger hole. The lowest note, produced by covering all the finger holes, was D; that produced by opening the lowest hole was E,

can be seen in plate VII, which shows Michel La Barre, a famous player and composer of the French court, with some of his colleagues. The English writer James Talbot also describes the flute d'Allemagne, naming Bressan as the maker of one of the two instruments he had examined. The German attribution, which dates back to the sixteenth century, perhaps resulted from its use as a military instrument by the German soldiers who were the successors of the earlier Swiss mercenaries, for an earlier name for the cross flute was the *Schweitzer-Pfeiff* or Swiss pipe. The German flute, however, was still not as popular as it was to become in the second half of the eighteenth century; ensembles were still small enough that the recorder was fully adequate to balance against a small string band, and musical styles were such that the recorder's tonal and musical qualities were more suited to what was generally

Plate V Rectangular virginals by Stephen Keene, London, 1668. FF-d³ without FF#, an unusually large compass, 1 × 8′. (*Russell Collection no. 8, Edinburgh University*)

Plate VI Musette du cour, anonymous, France. 2 chanters with 6 keys each, 4 drones in the shuttle. (*Pitt Rivers Museum, Balfour 117, Oxford University*)

Plate VII 'Michel La Barre
and colleagues', attributed to
Robert Tournières, *c.* 1710.
Three flutes of Hotteterre type
and viola da gamba. (*National
Gallery, London, no. 2081*)

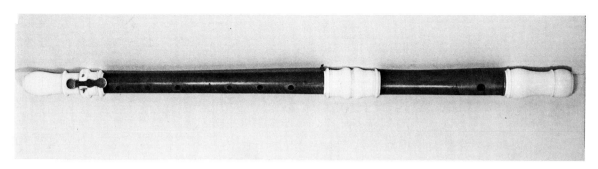

but by opening the key instead, the player obtained E flat or D sharp. Such chromatic keys had been used on a few of the reed instruments of the Renaissance, but they only came into common use with the introduction of the musette.

Just as many harpsichordists of the previous period demanded keyboards with split keys, so some flautists were worried about the effects of meantone tuning. One of these was Johann Joachim Quantz, one of the greatest flautists of his day, author of an important treatise on the instrument and on the performance of music in general; he was also the flute teacher and a resident composer to Frederick the Great. He insisted that his own and his royal master's flutes should have two keys in this position, one for E flat and the other, covering a slightly smaller or lower hole, for D sharp, and a few of these instruments survive. The one illustrated in plate 29 was the property of Frederick the Great; it has a fitted case of porcelain and is provided, as was the practice by this time, with a set of alternative upper-body joints. It dates from about 1750 and during the first half of the eighteenth century makers came to realise the advantages of dividing the one-piece body joint of the Hotteterre model flute into two separate joints, which, being shorter, could be reamed even more accurately and stored more easily. In addition, because pitch standards of the time varied considerably from place to place and because the flute, like all wind instruments, was affected in pitch by alterations in temperature but could not be retuned by turning a tuning peg like a string instrument, the provision of alternative upper-body joints, each of a slightly different length, allowed the player to keep in tune with other instruments. It was, of course, possible simply to draw the joints slightly apart, so increasing the length of the instrument and flattening the pitch, but because

the tenons were quite thick, unlike the thin metal tuning slides of modern instruments, which were not invented until the late eighteenth century, this created large chambers in the bore between the joints which threw the whole instrument out of tune. It is possible to insert specially made rings into the sockets to fill such gaps and, as Philip Bate points out, Quantz is known to have done so, but these also tend to be unsatisfactory and the normal solution, at least for the first half of the eighteenth century, was the use of a set of *corps de rechange* such as can be seen here and on plate IX.

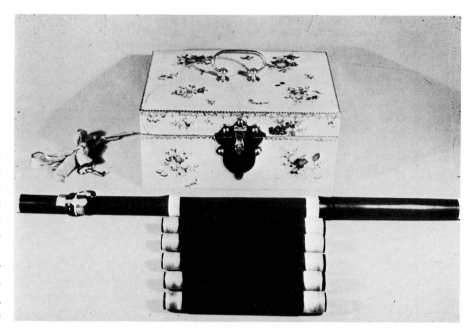

Only a very few makers, and these only in Germany, followed Quantz's example by fitting the enharmonic E flat and D sharp keys. All other makers provided only the one key and left it to the player to control the pitch by rolling the instrument slightly towards or away from the lip to produce whichever note was required. This was not particularly difficult to do and was, anyway, necessary for all other chromatic notes, all notes other than D, E, F sharp, G, A, B and C sharp, the natural notes of the instrument produced by opening the fingerholes in sequence from the bottom. These chromatic notes were obtained by cross-fingering, opening some holes but closing others below them, or else by half-covering a hole. It was because there was no hole below the E hole, which meant that it was impossible to cross-finger the E flat, and because it is more difficult to half-cover holes on the transverse flute than it is on the recorder, because of the angle at which it is held, that makers provided the E flat/D sharp key.

It is also possible that because the transverse flute is not responsive to such cross-fingerings, its acceptance as a normal instrument for serious music was delayed. It is not that cross-fingering does not work but that it has to be helped by altering the position of the embouchure to get the notes properly in tune. That this problem was recognised almost as soon as the instrument was invented is shown by plate VII. Philip Bate drew attention to the ivory flute held by the player nearest to the viewer, which has a duplicate hole in the middle of the body. He suggests that this might have been covered by the left little finger and used to produce a better G sharp than the usual cross-fingered note, and that there appears to be a hole just visible between the lowest two holes, which could be for the right thumb to give a better F natural than the conventional fingering, which is notoriously poor. No actual instruments from this period are known with such holes, although one late eighteenth century flute has the uppermost of these holes, and it must be assumed that despite the fact that they produced a better sound, the problems of keeping the holes covered when they were not required outweighed any advantages. The cross flute remained a one-keyed instrument and players obtained the chromatic notes as best they could, which meant that it was quite difficult to play music with several flats in the key signature, when almost every note would have to be humoured by rolling the embouchure on the lip. The oboe, on the other hand, was much easier to cross-finger successfully, and it may have been partly this difference between the two instruments that led to the immediate adoption of the oboe as the leading orchestral woodwind and the reluctance to regard the cross flute in the same light.

The Oboe

The oboe was an almost completely new instrument, created at the end of the seventeenth century, an instrument with a conical bore and played with a double reed, with a broad but sweet tone which blended incomparably well with the violins and which was ideal for the new indoor orchestras. However, because it was called *hautbois*, and because it replaced two other instruments, also of conical bore and also played with a double reed and, on top of that, also called *hautbois*, there was and still is a good deal of confusion.

In France *Les Douze Grands Hautbois* were the wind-band of shawms which played for royal processions and ceremonials, and although the term hautbois meant high woodwinds and specifically shawms, not all were high and not all were woodwind. The group included shawms of all sizes and curtals, which were more easily portable than the bass and great bass shawms, and also sackbuts. In England Charles II had instituted a similar group, also playing hautboys or wait-pipes, which again were shawms, for since he had spent most of his time of exile at the French court, he brought back the idea that only what was fashionable in Paris could be fashionable in London, and in music as well as in other matters the English court aped the French. The *Douze Hautbois*, the King's Hautboys, were the loud instruments which had been used in the Renaissance and it was their unsuitability for concerted music that led to the changes in all the woodwind instruments. Various makers began to produce refined shawms with a more moderate volume, among them, perhaps the first of them, was Haka, the expatriate Englishman living in Amsterdam; he retained his first name of Richard, but whether Haka was a Dutch version of an English name such as Harker, or whether he was of other, perhaps Bohemian, origin is unknown. He seems to have been the first to make an instrument known as the Deutsche Schalmei (plate 30, left), which is much nearer to an oboe than it is to a shawm (German, *Schalmei*), and he also made true oboes (next to the Schalmei in the plate). Johann Christoph Denner of Nuremberg made both shawms and true oboes; Jacob Denner, his son who signed his instruments I. Denner, made Deutsche Schalmeien and true oboes. As well as oboes of the normal treble size, both the Denners made larger oboes, including oboi d'amore, oboi da caccia, as can be seen in plate 31, and curtals. The Hotteterres made at least some oboes, though two out of the three surviving instruments are partly by other makers. Because of the lack of detailed information it is still not possible to date the introduction of the Deutsche Schalmei with any certainty; it may be earlier than the true oboe and it may be later. It is certain that by 1670 the new oboe was in use in Paris and that it spread within the following decade to other European centres.

The schalmei had a narrower bore than the old shawm, and it seems probable that the schalmei reed was slightly longer, allowing the player to grip more of it between his lips and thus reduce the volume to some extent as well as establishing more control over tone and tuning. The oboe has a still narrower bore and is played with a longer but narrower reed firmly gripped between the lips, which allows the player more control and a greater range than is possible with either the shawm or the schalmei. The tone of the oboe is quite different from that of either of the other instruments and the volume much quieter. The oboe became almost immediately an orchestral instrument and spread over Europe with such unusual speed because it blended so well with the string instruments. The blend was much better than that of the modern oboe because the reed, though longer and narrower than before, was by no means as narrow as that of the modern oboe, and as a result the tone was softer, warmer and broader than that which we hear today and the older oboe did not cut through the string sound like the modern one does.

Neither the treble shawm nor the treble schalmei had any keys, for although there was on the shalmei a hole below a fontanelle of the same type as was used to cover the key of the larger shawms, it never

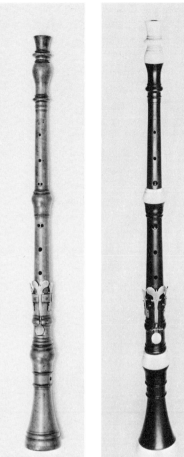

seems to have been covered with a key; some schalmeien have had a key inserted at a later period. The oboe on the other hand had three keys. One of these, with a long forked touch so that it could be taken by either little finger, was open-standing and, when closed, sounded the lowest note of the instrument, middle C. The others were shorter and stood closed, one on each side of the long key. Either of these, when opened, provided the E flat or D sharp. These keys were duplicated because they were mounted on the body of the instrument and not on a separate foot joint like that of the flute. They could not, therefore, be moved to suit those players who at this period had still not agreed on whether the right or the left hand should be the lower, and since either little finger might need to reach the key, the only way of providing for this was by duplication. There was no need for separate keys for E flat and D

Plate 30 HAUTBOYS. *Left to right:* Deutsche Schalmei by Richard Haka, *c.* 1680; oboes by Haka, *c.* 1680 (Ea6–1952), by Coenraad Rijkel, Haka's nephew, *c.* 1700 (Ea440–1933), and by Hendrik Richters, early 18th century (Ea584–1933); all made in Amsterdam. (*Gemeente Museum, Den Haag*)

sharp because the tuning of the oboe was more flexible than that of the flute. By making minute adjustments of pressure on the reed, the player could make sufficient alterations of pitch to play in any temperament. It was partly this control and the extent to which it allowed musicians to play expressively, that made the oboe so favourite an instrument with all composers almost as soon as it became available.

Like the recorder and other instruments, the oboe was made in different sizes, but instead of making the different sizes simply to have a range of instruments of similar tone colour but different pitches, some of the larger oboes were made so as to produce different tone colours. The oboe d'amore, a minor third lower than the normal oboe and the smallest instrument on plate 31, had a bulb bell, instead of the usual slightly flared open bell of the treble instrument, and thus a hollower, softer sound, often used by Bach for accompanying female voices. The oboe da caccia, a third lower still, was bent in the middle or, more usually, curved and had a flaring bell of wood or of brass like a small French horn bell. Surprisingly little is known of the ancestry of this instrument or

of its name, nor whether it was ever actually used in the hunt. It was built at the same pitch as three other oboes: the tenor oboe, which was in appearance simply a large oboe, with the same shape of bell as the treble instrument, merely enlarged proportionately to the rest of the instrument; a straight instrument, much like the tenor oboe in appearance but with a bulb bell; and the ancestor of the cor anglais (see plate 68), which, like the oboe da caccia, was built in a curved shape but with a bulb bell like that of the preceding instrument. The only one of the group, all of which can be seen on plate 31, to survive into modern times is the cor anglais, which is still a normal member of our orchestras.

Various suggestions have been made as to the origin of the bulb bell; one of the more likely is that advanced by Philip Bate, that quite simply it saved a vast amount of wood, for a flared wooden bell like that of the oboe da caccia when turned on a lathe leads to an excessive amount of waste as the wood is turned down from the open end to the socket into which the tenon at the end of the body fits. Another equally plausible reason, which Harry Vas Dias suggested to me, is that it also saves wood

Plate 31 LARGE OBOES. *Left to right:* oboe da caccia with brass bell by Johann Heinrich Eichentopf, Leipzig (*Musikhistoriska Museet, Stockholm, 170*); taille by Johann Christoff Denner, Nuremburg (1071), oboe da caccia with wooden bell by J. G. Bauer, Vienna (581), tenor oboe by Jacob Denner, Nuremburg (516), oboe d'amore by Johann Heinrich Eichentopf, Leipzig (73). (*Musikinstrumenten Museum, Berlin*)

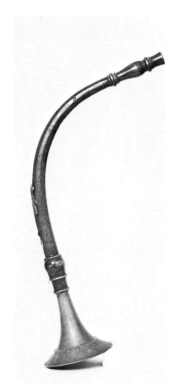
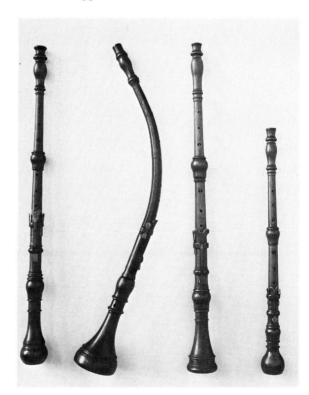

by reducing the length of the bell, for the acoustical effect of the bulb bell is to allow the instrument to be several inches shorter than it would need to be with an open bell. It is also true that the bulb bell affects the tone considerably, and this is another probable reason for its use.

The biggest problem with these four forms of the tenor oboe is to know how and for what they were used. Bach wrote a number of parts for oboe da caccia; he never wrote for cor anglais, but he did write a number of obvious tenor parts for an instrument he called the *taille*. Was taille a general name for tenor (he and other composers also used it for the viola, the tenor violin part), and was that part played by the oboe da caccia? Or was it a name which meant to Bach the tenor oboe or either the straight or the curved instrument with a bulb bell? We do not know, nor do we know which of these four types was used for the tenor parts in the great French oboe band, the reed group of the *Grande Ecurie*, for which Lulli, Couperin and many other composers wrote. Since there was such a group of oboes, with bassoons playing the bass line, and since the music for it demands the use of tenors, we can be sure that one or perhaps all of these patterns of tenor oboe were used. Much work remains to be done on the instruments of this period. Meanwhile, there is a general agreement that the curved instrument with a flared bell is the oboe da caccia and a tendency to refer to the instrument which looks like a large oboe as the tenor oboe and to the straight tenor instrument with a bulb bell as the taille and to hope that future research may prove these names to be correct. One further pattern of tenor oboe also existed but seems to be rather later, and it is therefore described in the next chapter where it is illustrated on plate 69.

Much of our knowledge of the oboe in England at this period comes from Talbot's manuscript, and he describes all three varieties: the English Hautbois or Waits (he describes treble and tenor); the Schalmey, which he describes as 'Saxon used Much in German Army, etc. Sweeter than Hautbois. Several sizes and pitches'; the French Hautbois, which is the true oboe, he describes in two sizes, both made by Bressan, the greatest woodwind maker in England of this period. As Anthony Baines points out in his notes to the wind section of the manuscript, not only is Talbot's reference here the only evidence that

Bressan made oboes, for none are known to survive, but Talbot is the only writer who distinguishes between the shawm and the schalmei; even today, thirty years after this portion of the manuscript was published, the majority of museums label their schalmeien as shawms and do not distinguish between them and the true shawms or, as Talbot called them, Waits.

The Bassoon

Talbot also distinguishes between the Fagot, which is disused, and the Basson, noting that the fingering for both is the same but that the Basson 'has four joynts whereas the Fagot is entire'. He distinguishes also between the Pedal or Double Basson and the Double Courtaut and notes that there are also treble and tenor courtauts. His Basson is, of course, our bassoon (plate 32) and his is the earliest reference to a double bassoon, though his instrument stands only a fourth lower than the normal instrument rather than an octave lower as is normal today. His Fagot and Courtaut both refer to the curtal (*Choristfagott* or *Doppelfagott* in German, according to size) and this was the old one-piece instrument, entire as he describes it, the earlier version of the curtal shown in plate 23. Just as the old shawms were dying out except for street work and similar occasions, so the curtal was on the way out, the bassoon in four joints being as much better in tone and tuning than the curtal as the oboe was than the schalmei and for the same reason: the separate joints made it easier to ream an accurate and careful bore. The bassoon had a much greater range than the curtal, and composers were quick to take advantage of this; there is a considerable literature of bassoon concertos and other solos, seldom played today unfortunately, but awaiting the attention of virtuoso bassoonists, for some of it is by no means easy to play, something that can also be said of much of the orchestral bassoon repertoire of this period. In Bach's Mass in B minor, for example, everybody notices the horn soloist in *Quoniam tu solus sanctus*, for the writing is elaborate and the horn, especially at that period, was a conspicuous instrument; however, the accompanying parts for two bassoons are, if anything, more difficult and must have been more difficult still on the instrument with four keys that was used at that time. Talbot's bassoon had only three keys and

Plate 32 Two bassoons by Johann Christoff Denner, Nuremburg, late 17th century. *Right:* showing the finger holes (2970); *left:* showing the thumb holes and keys (2969). (*Musikinstrumenten Museum, Berlin*)

49

Plate 33 *Left:* bassoon; *right:* contrabassoon, both by Thomas Stanesby junior, London. The bassoon is dated 1747 (*William Waterhouse*) and the contrabassoon 1739 (*National Museum of Ireland, Dublin*)

probably resembled the two bassoons shown in plate 32, both of which are by J. C. Denner and one of which is turned to show the finger holes and the other the thumb holes.

The bassoon is peculiar in that it has a tube with six finger holes, like all other woodwind instruments, but this takes the instrument, starting at the reed, only through the crook or bocal, down through the wing joint and into the butt. Then, via a U-bend at the bottom of the butt, the tube comes up again into the long joint and on up out of the bell, the addition of which is the most obvious change from the old curtal. All this second section from the butt upwards is found only on the bassoon and the curtal, and since the player's fingers are fully occupied by covering the holes in the first section, in the wing joint and the downward section of the butt, any finger holes in the second section have to be manipulated by the player's two thumbs with whatever help can be provided by the lower little finger. The little finger on even the curtal and the earliest bassoons was provided with a key to cover the lowest hole on the down-tube in the butt, sounding the low F (plate 32, right) and this, like the C key on the oboe, was forked so that it could be reached by either little finger, depending on whether the player kept the right or the left hand above the other. Then, as may be seen on the left of plate 32, while the lower thumb was responsible for one hole on the upward tube of the butt, the upper thumb controlled a hole in the long joint and two keys, one above the hole and one below it, thus producing the low B flat out of the bell, the C by opening the upper key, the D by uncovering the hole and the E with the lower key.

It must be remembered that the pitch of notes produced by finger holes depends not only on the diameter and the position of the finger holes along the tube, but also upon the length of the finger holes through the wall of the instrument. This length will normally depend upon the thickness of the material of which the instrument is made. One of the problems with the bassoon is that the tube is long, thus requiring a wide spread of finger holes, whereas the spread of the human hand is limited, and it is for this reason that the bassoon has a wing joint. The outer orifices of the finger holes can be placed close enough together to allow the player to cover them with his fingertips and the holes can then diverge

through the thickness of the wing, the uppermost hole slanting sharply upwards, the middle hole running fairly straight and the lower slanting sharply downwards, so that they are somewhere near their correct positions on the bore of the instrument. The holes in the long joint, however, are drilled straight through a comparatively thin piece of wood, for the distant ones are covered by keys, and it is one of the minor musical miracles that an instrument with some quite wide holes a few millimetres deep and some narrow holes several centimetres long can produce a tone which is even, homogeneous and does not change disastrously from one part of its compass to another, and is reasonably well in tune.

By the second quarter of the eighteenth century, designs and patterns of wood turning had changed somewhat, as had, to some slight extent, the bore profiles. The most obvious difference between the Denner bassoons on plate 32 and the Stanesby Junior bassoon on the left of plate 33 is that whereas the earlier makers thought of each joint of the instrument as a separate entity, turning it accordingly on the lathe perhaps to make the differences between the curtal and the bassoon all the more obvious to the eye, later makers were concerned to make the instrument as easy to hold and play as possible, seeing the whole instrument as a single entity and designing the wing joint so that it would lie snugly against the long joint. By this time a fourth key had been added, for the low A flat, to make the four key bassoon for which Bach and Handel wrote.

An instrument which seems to be unique and which was probably made for Handel's *L'Allegro* and used again in the *Music for the Royal Fireworks* is the contrabassoon dated 1739, also by Stanesby Junior, which survives in Dublin and which is also illustrated on plate 33. This sounds an octave below the ordinary bassoon and is simply a normal bassoon of the period but twice the normal length. Both Stanesby Junior and his father are known to have made such instruments, no others of which are known to survive, but all other contrabassoons until the end of the century were, like Talbot's, only a fourth, or occasionally a fifth, below the ordinary bassoon.

The Chalumeau

It was in this period that a completely new instrument appeared, the chalumeau, for which a number of composers wrote a few parts. It seems to have been a small instrument of limited range and usefulness, and one problem in identifying it has been that chalumeau is an indeterminate name, obviously the French equivalent of shawm and of Schalmei, and a name that has at various times been associated with a variety of instruments made from, or played with, a reed. It is generally assumed that the instrument of this name for which Handel, Telemann and others composed was a small ancestor of the clarinet, looking like a descant/soprano recorder but played with a single reed like that of the clarinet, and such an instrument can be seen on the left of plate 34. There are seventeenth century references to an instrument called in English the Mock Trumpet, and it has been convincingly suggested by Thurston Dart that this was the English name for the same instrument and that the chalumeau was known in Britain around the turn of the century. Certainly the clarinet derives its name from the fact that it sounded like a trumpet in the high register, for which the Italian term is *clarino* and the diminutive, appropriate to a small instrument, would be *clarinetto*. Modern reconstructions of such an instrument have been made on which it is possible to play all the surviving chalumeau parts, and they are convincing enough to suggest that these suppositions as to its identity are correct.

The Clarinet

By about the year 1700 the chalumeau had been increased in size and in range and the clarinet, the right-hand instrument on plate 34, had been invented. This invention is due to J. C. Denner, the maker of the instrument illustrated. Apart from the increase in size, the main distinction between chalumeau and clarinet is that the chalumeau played either in its bottom register, without overblowing, so that its range was restricted to an octave or a little over, or in its upper register, but not in both. The clarinet's thumb key was moved so that it could be used as a speaker-key to break the air column at the correct acoustical point. The instrument could then overblow and the gap in the compass between the chalumeau register and the overblown register (see below) was filled by the use of a thumb hole, a key for the upper index finger and a hole for the lower little finger drilled in a movable foot joint like that of the recorder.

The basic problem which had to be surmounted before the clarinet could become a useful instrument was that its bore was cylindrical and that it was blown with a reed. The effect of this combination is two-fold: the sound produced is much lower than it would be if the bore were conical; and the overblown pitch is a twelfth higher than the basic pitch, instead of an octave higher as it would be on a conical instrument. The low pitch of the basic register has always been one of the great advantages of the clarinet, both for beauty of sound and for compactness, for the clarinet is half the length that a flute would need to be in order to produce the same notes. The fact that it overblew a twelfth inhibited its adoption in its early years, for unless there are extra finger holes or keys, there will be a gap between the basic register and the overblown register. It was because of this gap that music of only minor importance was written for the chalumeau, for no composer will trouble to write much for an instrument if he must keep remembering that certain notes cannot be played, and it was by filling this gap with the holes and the keys described that Denner created the clarinet.

The early clarinet looked very much like a recorder, apart from the two keys at the upper end and the mouthpiece with its single reed. During the first quarter of the eighteenth century the bell was increased in size, but there was still one note missing from the range: the lowest note on the instrument was F, overblowing a C, and the highest note of the basic register was B flat, and there was no practicable way of producing the B natural between the two. This note was obtained by lengthening the bell still further and by fitting a third key which could be turned to make it accessible to either the left little finger when the left hand was the higher, or the left thumb if the right hand were the higher, and this can be seen on plate 35, which shows two such instruments, one from the front and one from the back. With this key the compass of the clarinet was complete. However, the intonation of the chromatic notes still left much to be desired, for the clarinet is even less responsive to cross-fingerings than the flute, and it may have been partly for this reason that composers were slow to adopt its use. Another reason may have been that it was still new and unfamiliar and probably not widely available, for com-

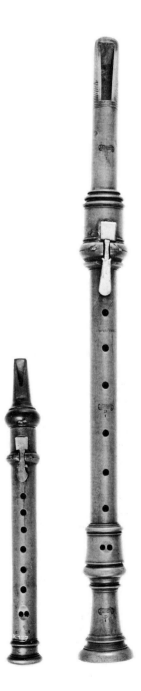

Plate 34 *Left:* chalumeau marked Stuehnwal, *c.* 1700 (Mu 137); *right:* clarinet by Johann Christoff Denner, Nuremburg, *c.* 1705 (Mu 136). (*Bayerisches Nationalmuseum, München*)

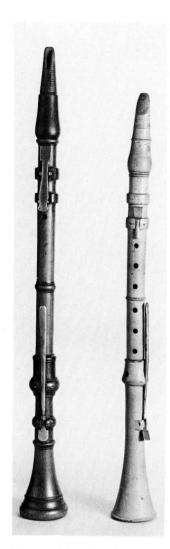

posers normally wrote for a specific group of players and they tended quite naturally to write only for the instruments which those players possessed; moreover, they were reluctant to write for instruments with whose capabilities they were unfamiliar. Certainly it was not until the next period that there appeared any great quantity of clarinet music.

Brass Instruments

The Horn

The horn was slowly becoming accepted as a member of the orchestra, though still usually only as a special instrument for large and festive occasions or to suggest to the audience the hunting field or the season of the year when huntsmen could be expected to be galloping across the fields to the accompaniment of rousing choruses of horns. It was blown with the bell held upwards and its great length, some four metres of brass or copper tubing coiled in a circle (plate 36), made it easy to play in the upper register without the quietness so characteristic of the high register of the trumpet. As a result, with the flaring bell helping to project its sound at the audience, it had a tendency to drown the other instruments, and one can see from their scores that composers as a rule took care to avoid this. A comparison of the first two *Brandenburg Concertos* is instructive in this regard. In the second concerto, the trumpet is very much one of the concertino, the small group of soloists who exchange among themselves the main melodic parts of the work, and the fact that the other

Plate 35   Two three-key clarinets, one by R. Baur, Vienna, in C, showing the back (*Rück Collection* MIR 425), the other anonymous in E flat showing the front (MI 150). (Both *Germanisches National-museum, Nürnberg*)

Plate 36   French horn in F at 18th century pitch, by William Bull, London, 1699. Copper with brass garland and original ivory mouthpiece. (*Carse Collection, Horniman Museum, London, 14.5.47/307*)

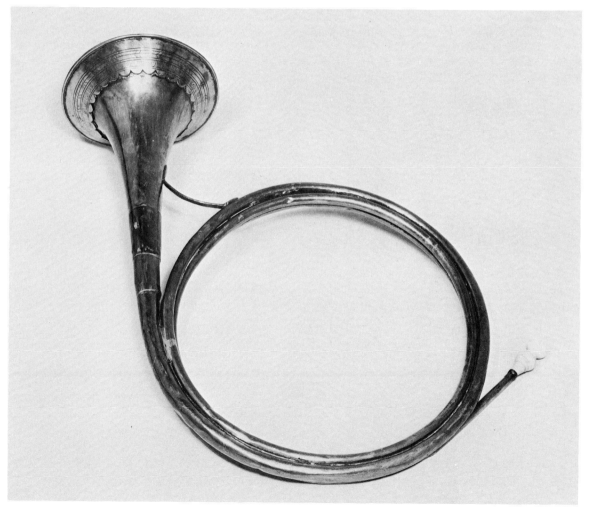

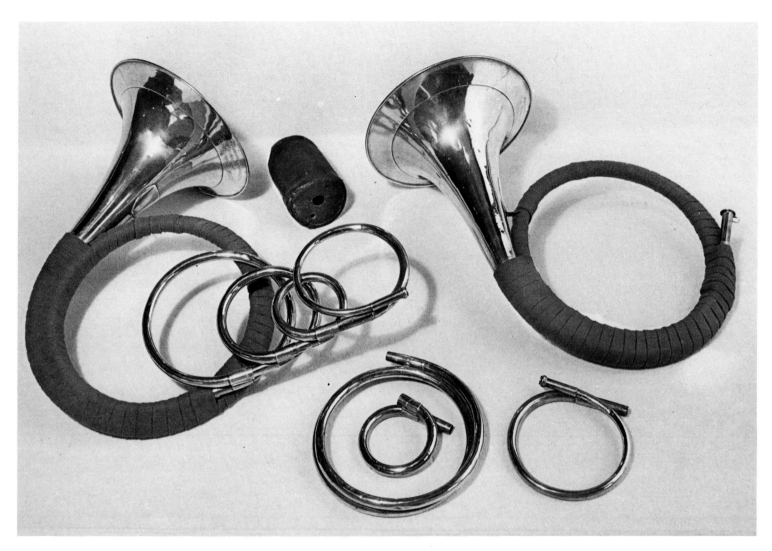

members of this group are recorder, oboe and violin indicates how quietly the natural trumpet of the period could and did play; trumpet and recorder were equal in volume, something that we forget today when we hear the modern piccolo jazz cornet, which now masquerades under the name of a trumpet, drowning the Boehm-system transverse flute even though that latter instrument is far more powerful than a recorder. On the other hand, in the first concerto the horns are not an integral part of the concertino; the slow movement is written for a solo oboe and a solo violin with ripieno (the main body of the orchestra) and the other movements are written for a group of strings led by a solo violin, a group of oboes and a pair of horns, and the horns

belt out their hunting calls and their running passages against the rest of the players. In the only movement in which the horns play as soloists, all three oboes have to play together in unison to counter them. Similarly in Handel's *Music for the Royal Fireworks* the three horns are well able to combat the united forces of the other players, including three trumpets and timpani and, in two movements, the side drums, and not only are the side drums specified in the plural but it was quite clear that more than one pair of timpani were expected—probably one or two pairs of normal instruments and a pair of double drums. Only in 'La Paix' does Handel beg the horns to play quietly and to blend with the other instruments.

Plate 37 Pair of orchestral horns with master crooks, couplers, tuning bits and mute, by John Christopher Hofmaster, London, *c.* 1735. (*Shaw-Hellier Collection, Warwickshire Museum*)

Horns were beginning to be regular members of military bands and there were players enough that not only were they available for orchestral use when required but travelling virtuosi were starting to appear, usually in pairs, giving concerts in various centres, with the result that makers began producing purpose-built instruments for such use. In the hunting field the wide, open coil had been useful, for players could ride with the hoop over the head and one shoulder, but in the orchestra such a design was inconvenient. Instruments were made rather more tightly coiled, such as that by William Bull in plate 36, which took up less space.

The main inconvenience of such a design was that the instrument could produce the harmonic series of only one key. Figure 2 is written, as is conventional for brass music, in the key of C, but the sounds that a horn would produce when the player read those notes would depend upon the length of the tube. A horn four-and-a-half metres long would produce them a tone higher, in the key of D; played on a tube some four metres long, they would come out a fourth higher than written, in the key of F. As a result, the player who was asked to go on a river picnic and play Handel's *Water Music* would need to know whether he was to play the F major *Water Music* or the D major, to avoid taking two horns with him. Musicians are as averse to taking needless trouble as the next man and so a solution was adopted which allowed players to take one horn and some extra lengths of tubing which would put the instrument into whichever key was desired. To achieve this, the tubing was cut and the main body of the instrument coiled rather more tightly; separate coils, called crooks, were inserted between the body of the horn and the mouthpiece (plate 37) so that the pitch could be changed by using a shorter or a longer crook. Such crooks had been known for the past century on trumpets and trombones and can be seen on plate 18 beside both those instruments, but since the horn had not then been used in serious music, they had not been applied to that instrument. Moreover, since the trumpet and trombone were made of cylindrical tubing, it had been quite easy to make a crook of tubing of the same diameter with a socket at one end for the mouthpiece and a slight taper at the other to fit into the body of the instrument. The horn, on the other hand, was conical in bore so that any crook would have to taper from the diameter of the mouthpiece shank up to the diameter of the tubing at the point at which it had been cut, something which required rather more skill and precision. It may have been the need for such skill, and the occasional lack of it, which induced some players to continue to use the old one piece instrument in the orchestra, as can be seen in many pictures. The result is that although when we find a horn today with separate crooks we can be certain that it was an orchestral instrument, we can never be sure whether such instruments as that by Bull shown in plate 36 are for hunting or for orchestral use. It may indeed have been that they were used for both purposes; certainly on the Continent the players were the same —the huntsmen moved indoors when required for the orchestra in the prince's salon. We can, however, be certain that horns such as that shown in plate 38 were hunting horns, for these multiply-wound instruments with a bell that can be unscrewed were designed so they could be carried in a huntsman's hat.

The existence of English horns such as those shown on plates 36 and 38 and other surviving instruments suggests that hunting may have been as ceremonial an affair in Britain around the year 1700 as it was in Germany, Austria, Hungary and France, which were the main centres for the use of long, coiled horns in the field. Such instruments are needed only if fanfares, and especially fanfares played by a group of players, are part of the accompaniment to the hunt. Instructions to men or hounds can be as easily transmitted by a simple short instrument, such as is used in Britain today, as by a long one, and the short instrument is far more portable and less susceptible to damage when the huntsman falls from his horse, as all are bound to do now and again. It is when the company is assembled round the fruit of the chase, and when there are a number of people equipped both with horns and the skill to sound them that the short horn, capable of only one or two notes, reveals its deficiencies. Such choruses of triumph, or of mourning for the slain beast, can be effective only when players can produce different notes either simultaneously in sonorous chords or in succession in melodic flourishes, or more usually both together, and for this a tube that is long enough to sound at least the first eight tones of the harmonic series is required. The amount of training received by an army bugler allows him to sound the first six, cocasionally eight, partials on a tube less than a metre-and-a-half long. The prolonged studies of a modern professional trumpeter permit him to achieve up to perhaps the twelfth harmonic on a tube of the same length. A modern horn player, on the other hand, with a tube over three-and-a-half metres long and equivalent training should be able to reach to at least the twentieth harmonic. This greater ease in producing the higher harmonics on a longer tube is reflected in the history of the horn.

Plate 38 Hunting horn in D at 18th century pitch, close-coiled with removable bell, in original case. Anonymous English, c. 1705. (*Carse Collection, Horniman Museum, London, 14.5.47/254*)

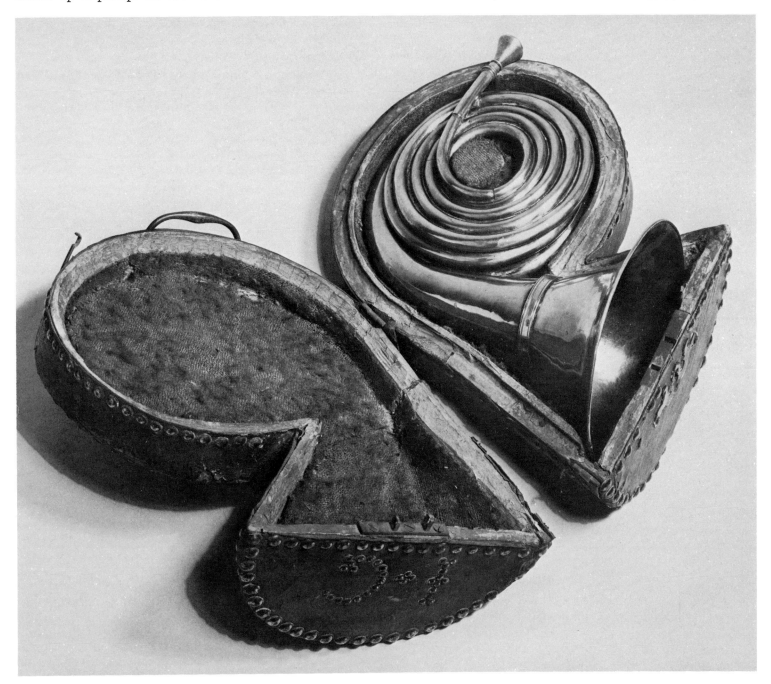

To enable a man, especially a man who was being bounced around while riding a horse on a frosty morning, to sound more than the first four harmonics, which were about all that was required of a cavalry trumpeter on his two-metre tube, the horn was extended to its eighteenth century length of between three-and-a-half and four-and-a-half metres, according to the pitch desired. The resulting ease with which the higher harmonics could be produced, and with sufficient freedom and power for the sound to ring through the woods and across the hills, encouraged the use of the horn in the orchestra, but only with the care and in the circumstances already described.

The Trumpet

The High Baroque saw the summit of trumpet virtuosity. Playing of such skill and over such a range has never been equalled except in the days of the great American jazz players of the first half of the twentieth century, and they had various mechanical aids which made the task somewhat easier. The trumpet itself was little changed from the previous period, the bell being slightly narrower, though this change, and the greater skills acquired over the period by manufacturers in maintaining the exact proportions of the tubing, rendered control of the upper harmonics far more certain. The finest instruments were still made in Nuremberg, many by the various members of the Haas family, such as that by Johann Wilhelm Haas shown in plate 39, though the superb instruments of the great English goldsmith trumpet makers, such as that shown in plate 40, rival them in quality and often excel them in beauty. On these instruments skilled players were able to play up to the twenty-fourth harmonic and to range

with the utmost lightness and facility from the eighth to the twentieth. From the tenth harmonic upwards the trumpet was a fully chromatic instrument, for the eleventh harmonic could be lipped up to F sharp or down to F natural at will, and the thirteenth to A flat or A natural. Since natural trumpets were seldom if ever called for in music in minor keys, the E flat between the ninth and the tenth harmonics was seldom required, though it was possible to lip down to it, nor were the C sharp or D flat between the eighth and the ninth often written. Thus the natural trumpet was able to play any notes normally required in its main solo range, and this without any artificial aids but simply through the skill of the player. Such skills were acquired, in Germany at least where we know more details of the process, through long and carefully controlled apprenticeship, where only an established master trumpeter was permitted to take apprentices and where the number of such apprentices was strictly limited. Some priority was given to the orphans and children of other trumpeters, for the trumpeters' guilds, which controlled such matters, were concerned for the welfare of the widows and orphans of their members as well as for the strict control of membership and numbers of the guild.

It is clear from written records that some players acquired greater skill than others, for not all players could adequately control the eleventh harmonic, which stands exactly halfway between F and F sharp (hence the half sharp drawn before it in figure 2), and a number of writers complain that this note was frequently out of tune. Nevertheless, the freedom with which composers wrote either F or F sharp, instead of adapting their melodic lines to avoid it, indicates that most players were able to

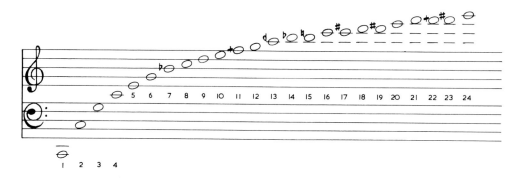

Fig. 2 The first 24 of the harmonic series.

56

Plate 39 Trumpet by Johann
Wilhelm Haas, Nuremburg,
c. 1700; brass. (*Germanisches
Nationalmuseum, Nürnberg,
MI 398*)

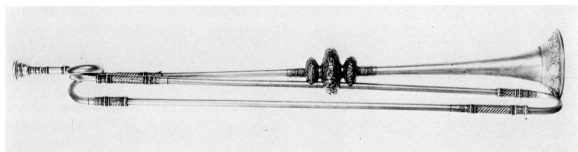

Plate 40 Trumpet in D with
C crook by William Bull,
London, late 17th century;
silver but not hall-marked. The
lower picture shows the same
instrument dismantled, the
bell-yard above, mouth-yard
in the centre and middle-yard
below. (*Ashmolean Museum
Oxford*)

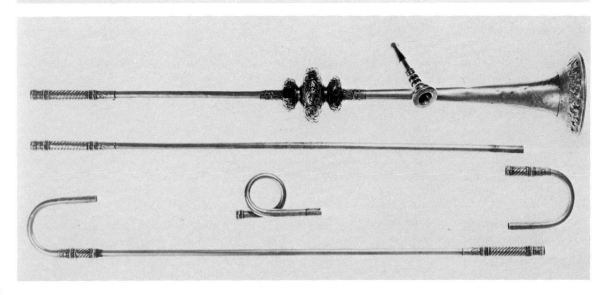

control it to their satisfaction. No composer writes notes which he knows are going to be played out of tune, and it is axiomatic that composers do not write music in the hope that some future invention may render it tolerable; all music is written for its own time and for the musicians and the instruments available at that time. Modern players of the early music revival, who have not undergone such apprenticeships and who are economically unable to devote the necessary hours of incessant practice in order to acquire the techniques of the High Baroque, tend to depend upon finger holes, which act as speaker-holes, breaking the air column and so allowing them to produce a subsidiary harmonic series in which these notes are in tune, a series which is much weaker in volume and deficient in tone quality. That only a very few original trumpets survive pierced with such a hole (one is shown on plate 77, but it is clear that the hole was not used for this purpose) indicates that such a practice was not adopted in the eighteenth century. At least one modern trumpeter, the late Joseph Wheeler, has shown that these skills can be revived today, without the need for such finger holes, by those who are willing to devote the necessary time and trouble to acquire them.

We know that this technique of clarino playing (it should, perhaps, be emphasised that the word clarino refers to a part of the range of the trumpet, from about the 8th harmonic upwards, and, by extension, to music written in that range and to the players of such music; there was no such instrument as a clarino, for all trumpeters played on the same trumpets) was taught by apprenticeship because Altenburg's treatise, though written late in the eighteenth century, looks back with nostalgia and regret for the all-but forgotten days when such skills were employed and were properly taught, and he describes the procedure in some detail. The trumpeters' guild was still sufficiently powerful in the early eighteenth century that if anyone who was not a member of the guild were caught playing a trumpet, both his instrument and his front teeth were smashed so that never again would he usurp the privileges reserved to his betters, the members of the guild. These privileges were very real; trumpeters and timpanists, for both instruments were always used together and the players of both were therefore members of the same guild, had rights and privileges which were denied to other players, and they were the highest caste of musicians attached to such princely houses and other establishments as had acquired the privilege of maintaining a corps of trumpeters. This privilege was not generally available and composers such as Bach were severely restricted as to the occasions on which they might include trumpets and drums in their music.

At least one trace of such restriction survives in Britain today: no orchestra playing at an official function in the Guildhall of the City of London may include trumpets and timpani unless the Lord Mayor of London is present in person. There is little other evidence of such restrictions in Britain nor do they seem to have existed in France. However, the use of trumpets and timpani has ever been an appurtenance of royalty and aristocracy, and this is indicated in France and Britain by the survival in Britain of more trumpets of silver or with silver garnishes than of plain brass, and by the almost total absence of any such instruments in France, for which we have the Revolution to thank; at the same time as it swept away the aristocracy it seems to have melted down, when of silver, and broken up, when of brass, such evidence of their pomp and their power.

The surviving British instruments, one of which by William Bull is shown on plate 40, are magnificent instruments as might be expected when one realises that, as Maurice Byrne has shown, their makers were all entered as goldsmiths as well as instrument makers. The massive ball on the bell-yard is a device which served a multiple role, for as well as enhancing the beauty of the instrument, it covered the joint in the tubing where the cylindrical body gave way to the conical bell, it gave the player a place to grip the instrument and it also held together the bell-yard and the mouth-yard. As Eric Halfpenny was the first to point out, the joints of the tubing of the early eighteenth century trumpets were not soldered together as they are on modern trumpets (and as, in fact, they are on far too many early eighteenth century trumpets today, as the result of ignorant repair), but consisted of three straight yards linked with two U-bends, which fitted together by tenon and socket joints in exactly the same way as the contemporary woodwind, probably with the use of wax to keep them airtight rather than the waxed thread used on the woodwind to lap the tenons. Both photographs in plate 40 show the same instrument, the lower with its parts separated in this way. The German trumpets were provided with a wooden spacing block between the mouthpipe and the bell-yard, the whole lashed together with cord for stability in use, and the front bow of the tubing was attached to the bell by a twist of soft wire which passed through a small hole in the rim of the bell. On the British instruments, with their massive balls, the ball was grooved or, as can be seen in more than one example, pierced as in the instrument on plate 40, to allow the passage of the mouth-yard. Such a construction, combined with the angle at which the mouth-yard was set, is so solid and firm in use that no wooden block was needed and a binding of twine sufficed to hold it together; yet it allowed the instant dismantling of the trumpet for storage or for transport when accidental damage might be feared.

Experience of playing both German and English trumpets of this period shows differences between them greater than those just of appearance. One has a strong impression of greater power, of greater solidity of tone on the English trumpets, as though they were designed to function at full volume up to at least the twelfth and perhaps the sixteenth harmonics, whereas the German trumpets seem to play best in the upper register with a quiet and intimate chamber tone. This is to some extent borne out by differences in the trumpet music of the two countries, where one might contrast the English 'Trumpet Tune', so frequently encountered in the music, especially the theatrical music, of Purcell and his contemporaries and successors, and so often copied for the trumpet stop on the organ, with the many chamber concerti and other works of German and Italian composers. One could also say that exuberant works such as Handel's *Water Music* and *Fireworks Music* suit the English trumpet far better than the German, which is a point to be borne in mind today when good copies of German trumpets, such as those by Meinl und Lauber, are easily available whereas Christopher Monk's copies of English trumpets, which are the first to have appeared, are only very recently on the market. One must admit, however, that such works as the third and fourth Orchestral Suites by J. S. Bach, and indeed some of his great choruses, suggest that the German trumpets may have been equally able to hold their own with full volume against almost any competition. The competition in these works was somewhat less than that which Handel's trumpeters had to contend with and it is suggested that this difference in forces may still be sufficient to indicate that there was a real and desired tonal difference between the two nationalities of trumpet.

The Tuning Fork

It is to one of the most famous of Handel's trumpeters that we owe the invention of one of the simplest and yet most essential of musical 'instruments'. Nothing, it would seem, could be simpler than a tuning fork, but without John Shore's invention of this useful device, how difficult it would be to tune any instrument! Before this invention, the only available standard was the pitch pipe, a single small wooden pipe like an organ pipe, as can be seen in plate 41, but with an adjustable piston which could be set to the desired length. However, it is difficult to set the position of the piston absolutely exactly and, as any recorder player knows, the strength with which one blows affects the pitch, as does any variation in temperature, so that the note produced by a pitch pipe can only be approximate. What is more, in order to produce this approximate pitch, the player has to lay down his instrument, pick

Plate 41 Pitch pipe, anonymous. (*Carse Collection Horniman Museum, London 14.5.47/194*)

up the pitch pipe, adjust its length, apply it to his mouth and blow. With a tuning fork, he has only to strike it on a suitable surface (his own knee is always the best) and hold it to his ear. There are few surviving forks that can be dated with any certainty; that illustrated on plate 42 gives a pitch so low that, combined with the inherent improbability of anyone requiring a fork for B natural, it is assumed to be an early eighteenth century pitch middle C.

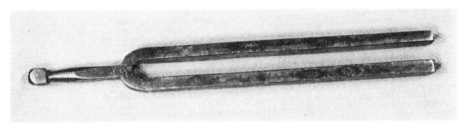

Plate 42 Tuning fork, anonymous, probably early 18th century. Sounds 244 hz, a low-pitch middle C. (*Author's Collection VII 186*)

The Timpani

Although still regarded as bass trumpets musically, the timpani were much more formally recognised than before, their parts being written into the music, which was comparatively rare in the previous period when it was left to the player to improvise a part from the lowest trumpet part. Even now a timpanist would be expected to improvise in fanfares and entrances and exits (German *Aufzüge* and *Auszüge*), but when the trumpets were used in threes and fours in the orchestra, as they normally were in Germany, or in twos and threes as was more usual in England and elsewhere, it became customary for the composer to write at least the skeleton of the part. It was still very much a part of the tradition that the timpanist should ornament his part with decorative flourishes, both of his arms and his music, many of which were deliberately designed to be impressive to the watcher as well as to the hearer; the timpanist in the orchestra retained some of the showmanship still shown by baton-twirling drum-majors, and many pictures and engravings of this and the following century show the timpanist at the back of the orchestra with his sticks high in the air. Some composers, of course, preferred to write exactly what they wished to hear and when one considers the elaborate and precise ornamentation of the melodic parts which J. S. Bach carefully wrote into his scores, one has the strong feeling that what he wrote for the timpani also was what he expected

the timpanist to play. Handel, on the other hand, quite clearly expected an elaboration of the part, a tradition that was well-recognised in the next generation, as can be seen by comparing Handel's original simple timpani parts with the more elaborate versions which Mozart wrote out in his re-orchestrations of such works as *Messiah*.

The timpani themselves were normally still quite small and quite shallow (plate 43). In the army, and especially in the artillery where it was normal to carry the drums on a horse-drawn chariot rather than on horse-back, much larger instruments were often used. These were known as double drums because they were about twice the size of ordinary drums. The records survive of the numerous occasions when Handel was allowed to borrow a pair of double drums from the royal Armouries, but the drums themselves have disappeared, perhaps, as Farmer suggests, lost in the fire at the Tower of London in 1841. When Charles Cudworth published John Marsh's *Advice to Young Composers of Instrumental Music* of about 1806 we discovered that the double drums, by that date at least and possibly earlier, were much more widely used than Farmer's evidence would suggest. Only one surviving pair of double drums is known (plate 44) and these drums show all the characteristics of the normal early eighteenth century timpani, save for their great diameters; the plate shows them with a pair of the normal size, though of rather later date. The square tuning blocks turned with a loose key were the usual fitting until the end of the eighteenth century, and it was normal until well into the nineteenth century for the drums to rest on trestles when in use in the orchestra and to be provided with small feet for when they were put on the ground for storage, or even to have no feet at all, though this had the disadvantage that the bottom was easily dented unless they were stored upside-down.

One little-recognised feature of eighteenth century drums, especially common in Germany, is the presence inside the drums of small metal funnels, similar in shape to horn or trumpet bells, fixed with the small end round the air hole in the base of the drum and projecting up into the kettle (plate 45). Little is known of their function, though recent research by Robert Sheldon (to whom I am grateful for permitting me to reveal his results) at the Smith-

sonian Institution in Washington has indicated that they have the effect of allowing the player to produce as good a tone when striking the centre of the skin as when he strikes the more normal playing spot some ten centimetres from the rim, something that would be a considerable advantage when playing on horse-back, for it is not easy to aim at exactly the right playing spot when riding a horse and executing showy movements of the arms.

Timpani sticks for most purposes consisted of wooden or ivory balls or discs on shafts of the same materials (some reproductions are shown on the drums in plate 44), though for occasional performances these may have been covered with a soft leather such as chamois. Certainly there was no use of sticks with soft felt covers of the types that are used today, and the sound of the shallow drums played with hard sticks was very clear, with a strong fundamental, and with none of the soft boom or muddy tone commonly heard today. The sound matched well the tone of the natural trumpets and gave them a secure foundation on which to build their parts. The attack was more definite than modern drums can hope to produce and the timpanist was able to duplicate all the tonguing techniques of the trumpeters.

The Flat Trumpet

The one piece of music that seems to be an exception to the general rule that when groups of trumpets were used one would also expect timpani is Purcell's *Funeral Music for Queen Mary* for four trumpets. Attempts by several eminent scholars to provide a timpani part have made it obvious that it is im-

possible to produce a part which would have any resemblance to authentic timpani parts of the period (the side drum is the only possible percussion instrument for this work). This is because the trumpets used were what Purcell called Flatt Trumpets. No such instrument survives and our only information on these comes from Talbot's manuscript, from whose description the instrument illustrated in plate

Plate 45 Funnel projecting
up into the interior of timpani,
anonymous, 18th century. The
timpani in plate 43 have
similar funnels inside. (*Private
Collection*)

46 was made. Talbot makes it clear that the flat
trumpets had a slide which allowed them to play
non-harmonic notes and thus play in a minor key,
and that the slide, unlike that of the sackbut, was in
the back bow and was moved backwards past the
player's ear. An instrument similar to this in design
was widely used in England in the nineteenth century
and will be described in the next book.

The Trombone

The sackbut itself was less and less used. Talbot says:
'The chief use of Sakbutt here in England is in
consort with our Waits or English Hautbois [the old
shawms]. It was left off towards the latter end of
K.Ch.2d & gave place to the Fr. Basson.' Its use did
survive on the Continent for accompanying voices
in church, a usage which continued through the
nineteenth century as can be seen in the scores of
many choral works, and also in the town bands,
especially in Germany, for playing or accompanying
chorales both in churches and out of doors, often
from the tower of the church or the town hall or
from a suitable balcony.

The Cornett

The use of the cornett was also dying out, partly
because of the increasing number of quiet woodwind
instruments which could play the same music with
fewer problems of intonation and skill, and partly
because of the increased range of the natural trumpet.
The great advantage of the cornett in its day had
been that it was a trumpet-type instrument with a
full melodic range, whereas the trumpet itself was
limited to the open notes of the harmonic series.
Once trumpeters began to climb into the upper part
of the series, where notes come close enough together to make melodic playing possible, there was
no need for a separate instrument to do the same
thing. It was still occasionally used, however, as can
be seen in Bach's cantata scores.

The Slide Trumpet and Horn

Another instrument appearing occasionally in the
music of this period was the *tromba da tirarsi*, only one
example of which survives (plate 47) and that of
rather earlier date. This, like the draw-trumpet of
the Renaissance, had a long tube attached to the
stem of the mouthpiece fitting telescopically inside

Plate 46 Reconstruction of
late 17th century flat trumpet,
by Philip Bate after Talbot's
description. Photographed
closed on the left and with the
slide in the back-bow drawn
out on the right. (*Bate
Collection, 717, Oxford
University*)

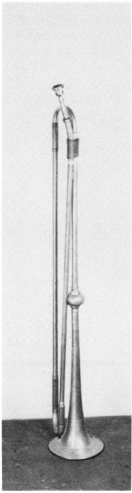

the first yard of the tubing. By drawing out this slide the fundamental pitch of the instrument could be altered, thus producing the natural harmonics of several pitches. With the slide right in, the instrument is in the D of the period; with it out some distance it would be in C sharp and further still in C, and so on, thus allowing the player to produce the notes between the harmonics of D in the lower part of the compass. In his recent book on brass instruments, A. C. Baines explains how such a slide can produce notes for which it is, in theory, too short. The slide trumpet seems to have been used mainly to accompany chorales and similar fairly slow music, probably because moving the whole weight of the trumpet in and out along the slide rendered it unsuitable for rapid shifts of position.

An instrument which is still a complete mystery, despite many attempts to identify it, is Bach's *corno da tirarsi*. It is easy to fit a telescopic slide to a trumpet, for the trumpet was made with long, straight yards into which a slide could be inserted. The horn, on the other hand, was coiled in a circle, and there is no evidence of an early eighteenth century horn with any straight cylindrical tubing. Various suggestions have been made, for example that the instrument was a slide trumpet or trombone with a deep, conical mouthpiece, but none has been convincing and certainly the use of a horn-type mouthpiece does not seem sufficient reason for the use of this name. The corno da tirarsi, like the lituus (and nobody supposes that Bach had a surviving Roman trumpet available to him) must remain for the present a mystery.

String Instruments

The Violin Family

Nobody has ever produced any reason to explain why the first fifty years of the High Baroque produced more great violin makers than any time before or since. Nevertheless, with the great masters who were the pupils of Nicola Amati in Cremona, such as Grancino, Guarneri, Rogeri, Ruggieri and Stradivari, to name only a few, and others such as Mathias Klotz in Mittenwald, Jacob Stainer at Innsbruck, Barak Norman in London, Joachim Tielke in Hamburg, Jan Boumeester in Amsterdam and many others, this was undoubtedly the greatest

era in the history of the violin. Within this period, and indeed up to the end of the eighteenth century, the greatest of these makers were held to be Amati and Stainer, with Stainer preferred by many players and other authorities as the better of the two. Both Amati and Stainer made their violins with highly arched bellies, with Stainer building the higher (plate 48, left), and their tone has been described by scholars such as David Boyden as flute-like, as distinct from the reedier, more oboe-like tone of the lower-bellied Stradivarius models (plate 48, right).

One of the problems in the design of the violin has always been that of combining a beautiful tone quality with a powerful volume. The deeper body provided by the highly arched belly produces a more beautiful but softer sound; the shallower body produces a more powerful volume but with somewhat less beauty. So long as great volume was not needed, the Amati and Stainer models reigned supreme. When, at the end of the eighteenth and the beginning of the nineteenth century, the first great public concert halls were built, the Stradivarius came into its own. Now, with our monster symphony orchestras and giant concert halls which have no natural resonance and are completely unsympathetic to the sound of string instruments, quite unlike the nineteenth century halls such as the Leipzig Gewandhaus and the Amsterdam Concertgebouw, whose resonance added a glow to the tone of any instrument, the still more powerful instruments of makers such as Guadagnini are overtaking the Stradivari in popularity for soloists.

It must not be forgotten, of course, that nobody now living has ever heard a violin by any of these great makers. As we shall see in the next chapter, every single surviving example has been so radically reconstructed that although the comparisons cited above may be made and those made in the seventeenth and eighteenth centuries repeated, it must be remembered that the earlier writers were listening to different instruments from those that we hear today. The miracle is, in fact, that the work of these great masters was so wonderful that it has survived the butchery that has been carried out on their instruments and that these still, despite all that has been done to them, far outshine any violins that have been made since.

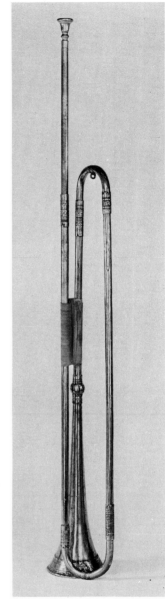

Plate 47 Slide trumpet by Huns Veit, Naumburg, 1651, shown with the sliding mouthpipe partly drawn out. (*Musikinstrumenten Museum, Berlin, 639*)

Plate 48 Violins by (*left*) Jacob Stainer, Absam, 1654 and (*right*) Antonius Stradivarius, Cremona, 1703. Both in modern state, but showing the models characteristic of these masters. (*Musikinstrumenten Museum, Berlin, 5176 and 4467*)

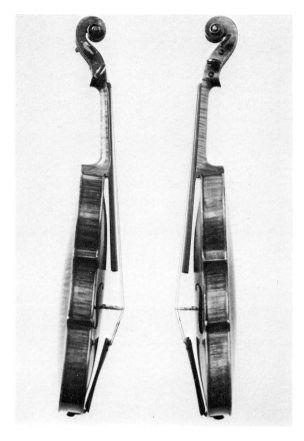

The violin finally became established in England in the seventeenth century. With the Restoration of the monarchy, it was not only the King that returned from France. Charles II and his entourage had lived long enough at the French court to become French in their manners and their taste and to realise, or at least to think, that Versailles and all that that implied was the proper home and style of a king and his court. If Louis XIV had his ballets with music by Lulli played by the *Vingt-Quatre Violons*, Charles must also have his orchestra of violins and French or Italian music masters to lead them and to compose for them in the French style. If the consort of viols was out of fashion at the French court, so would it be at the English court. If the solo concerto and the solo sonata were to be the fashionable form of music at the French court, so would they be at the English court. As a result, there was an abrupt change of musical styles in high society and in the instruments on which music was played. Viols were still heard and consort music still written, but only in and for

the old-fashioned houses that did not intend to follow the new and flighty fashions of the king and his courtiers. Purcell and Blow were the last great English composers for two hundred years; after their deaths, only the music of Monsieur Quelqu'chose or Signor Qualcun'altro or, under the Hanoverians, Herr Verschiedener, was heard in England. The Germans were more sensible; they preferred to hear music by German composers, provided of course that they wrote in the fashionable French galante style. Leipzig settled for Bach as its *Kapellmeister* only because better, to their taste, and more galante composers such as Telemann were not interested in the job.

The violin concerto became one of the most popular musical forms, either the solo concerto in which one player could pit his skill against an orchestra, or the concerto grosso in which the concertino of two violinists and a cellist played against the ripieno of the orchestra, and an almost equally popular musical form was the sonata in which a violinist was accompanied by the continuo or a solo harpsichordist. Many of these works were written by composers such as Tartini and Corelli who were themselves violin virtuosi, and this was a time when the virtuoso reigned supreme, for even if he had not written the concerto or the sonata himself, he was the composer of a good deal of the music which was actually heard. Composers were not expected to write every note of their music, and in fact those few who did so were ill thought of. A solo piece, in particular, was regarded as a vehicle for the performer to show his mettle, to ornament, to develop, so that often the musicians, who had their parts before them, were the only people present who knew what the composer had written; the hearers knew only what the performers played. And this is said with no derogatory implication; this is what was expected by all concerned and it is slowly becoming recognised today. When perhaps twenty years ago we might have heard a beautiful slow melody, today, at least with the better performers, we hear a filigree of scales and decorative passages flung out with the panache and *esprit* of a fountain, as these works were heard when they were new. And it was, of course, the violin that was the instrument best suited to such display.

The violin itself is an instrument of great and

restrained beauty, a wooden box shaped in beautiful and subtle curves, with a glowing varnished surface (plates II, 4, 48, 49 right and 88). The form of the instrument had already been firmly established, but each maker introduced slight differences so that, to the expert, the handiwork of each is instantly recognisable, which is not to say that the experts do not differ in their identification of the makers of various individual instruments; violin experts agree with each other no more often than do the experts in any other fields. Perhaps it was the influence of the decorations added to the music that inspired some makers, pre-eminent among them Joachim Tielke of Hamburg, to add decoration to the violins that played it, but it is more likely that both these forms of decoration were facets of the baroque, the spirit of the age. Certainly some violins, and also of course violas and cellos, were decorated to such an extent that the original form is almost lost below the exuberance of the maker, just as happened so often to the music of the composer.

There were a number of additional members of the violin family, many of them short-lived but all recognised and popular in their day. Small violins were made and used, the violino piccolo (plate 49, centre) for which Bach was to write in the first *Brandenburg Concerto*, an instrument which is difficult to identify today, for a small violin is a small violin. If the strings are tuned to the normal violin pitches, the instrument would be called a three-quarter size violin, used for teaching children not yet big enough to handle a full-size instrument. If, on the other hand, the strings are tuned to their normal tension, a higher pitch is produced and the instrument is a violino piccolo. Any violins identified as piccolos today are only so described as the result of guesswork, usually because they are of better quality and by better makers than one would normally give a child to learn on, but who is to say that the original owner did not believe that his children deserved the best?

Even smaller violins were used by dancing masters, but these were special instruments of special shape. Some had tiny bodies shaped like those of a violin, viol or other instrument, like the kit on the left of plate 49, which has a string length half that of a normal violin and is therefore tuned an octave higher. Others had small narrow bodies like a boat,

such as the pochette more often encountered in the seventeenth century and shown in the middle of plate 1 but which was still made in the later years of that century and possibly into the eighteenth. Both models were easily portable, the pochette slipping easily into the long pocket of the tail coat (hence its name), and produced a sound that although quiet was sufficient for a dancing class, a popular pastime in fashionable circles and in circles aping the fashionable. Both the terms, kit and pochette, were interchangeable in their own time, the former being the English and the latter the French names for the same instrument.

Another new instrument was the viola pomposa, a large version of the viola with a fifth string lower than the usual four (plate 50, left). Another was the violoncello piccolo, a small size cello with, again, a fifth string, but this time higher than the others so that the two instruments, although sometimes confused, are in fact easily distinguished. Confusion can arise with an instrument such as that shown on the

Plate 49 *Left to right:* kit by John Barrett, London, *c.* 1725; violino piccolo by Aegidius (Sebastian) Klotz, Mittenwald, 1776; violin by Giovanni Battista Gabbrielli, Florence, 1766. All in original condition except for the fingerboard of the kit. (*Carel van Leeuwen Boomkamp Collection, 2, 12 & 13, Gemeente Museum, Den Haag*)

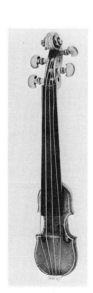

the violoncello, the bass of the family, remained rather more flexible in its details. Possibly it is sufficiently large, with a big enough resonance chamber, that small differences are not critical to the sound produced; possibly there was not sufficient agreement about just what sound should be produced; possibly also because its range was still so much greater than that of the violin, the precise size and shape of the resonance chamber was less critical. Whatever the reason, even among cellos by any one maker there is a considerable diversity of size and shape. The strings are tuned an octave lower than those of the viola, an octave and a half below those of the violin, with the lowest on the bass C, two lines below the bass clef and about as low as any bass singer can sing.

The Viols

Practically no new music was written for the viols in consort; there were exceptions in England, where Purcell and a few others wrote some superb music for this combination, but in Europe as a whole the concept of a group of viols was outmoded and old-fashioned. There were, however, sporadic attempts to save the viol from extinction. In France, for example, a new size of viol was invented towards the end of the seventeenth century, the *pardessus de viole* (plate 51), an instrument not much larger than a violin though rather deeper in the body—a characteristic of all the smaller viols when compared with the members of the violin family of similar string length. The pardessus remained popular for playing accompanied solos to the end of the eighteenth century even though it was too small to be very useful as a viol and of quite the wrong musical character to be any competition for the violin, which had swept all before it.

The one size of viol which did effectively survive and which reached new heights in the eighteenth century was the bass viol, the size normally referred to in English as the viola da gamba (plate VIII). Sonatas were written for it, Bach wrote some important solos for it in the Passions and the Cantatas as well as sonatas, and the great French virtuoso gamba player, Marin Marais, wrote several hundred superb works for it. It has also been suggested that where composers wrote for basso continuo, without specifying which bowed instruments were to play

right of plate 50, which appears to be a cello piccolo but which started life as a viola da gamba, was then converted into a cello, as happened to many viols as musical fashions changed, and then had a fifth string added, perhaps to play Bach's Sixth Suite for unaccompanied cello. There was also a violino pomposo, which was a violin with a fifth string below the four ordinary strings, an instrument which my son aptly described as a violin and a viola combined into one. While repertoire exists for all three of these instruments, the violoncello piccolo is much the most important of them, simply because Bach wrote the Suite for it. The viola in any size has never been an instrument for which many solo works have been written, perhaps because it has neither the brilliance of the violin nor the sonority of the cello, even though at all periods a few connoisseurs have valued it for its warmth of tone. Its middle voice has of course always been essential to music for the violin family.

Whereas the size and the shape of the violin was, during this period, to become fixed and standardised,

that line, the bass viol may well have been preferred even though today we automatically use a cello.

Certainly the instrument itself reached a final flowering, with many superb bass viols dating from this period, some by makers who are known chiefly as viol makers but many by makers whom we more frequently associate with the violin. So fine are these instruments that today, when we think of the bass viol, we tend to envisage it in the shape and form adopted at the end of the seventeenth and the beginning of the eighteenth centuries, just as we do the recorder. While this may be fair enough with the recorder, for this was the period in which much of the best music in its repertoire was written, it has led to a false impression of the viol, for although the solo music for bass viol was probably at its best at this time, the consort music belongs to the earlier period when the instrument was rather lighter in its construction and slightly different in its shape. It would not, for example, be appropriate to use one of the beautifully decorated instruments by Tielke, such as that shown in plate VIII, or those of Barak Norman or others of his contemporaries in early or mid-seventeenth century consort music.

Dilettante Instruments

This brings the problem of the decorative instruments to the fore again. They are frequently encountered in collections because they were built, in many cases, as collectors' pieces. Many were made to be exhibited in the *Kunstkabinet*, the show case of art works, rather than to be played on, and because the *Kunstkabinet* has survived as the nucleus of an art gallery or museum, the instruments have survived with it, while the ordinary playing instrument has either collapsed from use and age or has simply been tossed away once it became outmoded and of no further use. Some instruments manage to combine both functions, looking beautiful and sounding well, for there are parts of any instrument that can be decorated without much affecting the tone quality. On a string instrument, a decorated belly is almost certain to inhibit its vibration and thus detract from its tone quality. The back tends to vibrate rather less, for its prime function is to reflect the sound waves outwards towards the belly and the sound holes, and thus some decoration there may have less effect on the sound. Nevertheless, panels of inlaid or carved ivory will always cause the tone to be poorer than that of plain wood, and lutes or guitars with ivory backs will never sound as well as those with wooden backs. Decorating the ribs, the vertical walls of the soundbox, will have less effect on the sound, and this is one reason why guitars by makers such as Sellas often had ivory ribs; they looked well and did not affect the tone quality. Provided that it did not interfere with the smooth movement of the fingers and thumb from one note to another, decoration of the neck and the fingerboard, and beautifully carved scrolls and tailpieces, have no effect on the sound at all, and these are the most frequently encountered forms of decoration.

As far as keyboard instruments are concerned the type of instrument will generally determine whether decoration is advantageous or disadvantageous. The case of the comparatively lightly built Italian instruments is an important part of the sounding instrument and was seldom decorated, but because it was customary for the instrument to fit into an outer case, it was possible to decorate the outer case quite elaborately without affecting the tone quality. With the rather heavier northern European instruments it was another matter; the case was an important part of the sound-chain, but the instrument was built into it and could not be removed. Thus, if it were inhibited from free vibration by decorative panels, as on many *Kunstkabinet* examples from Augsburg, or by being plastered with jewellery or ivory marquetry, then almost certainly the sound would suffer. Thin paint on the soundboard obviously did not affect the sound, and paintings of birds, flowers and other decorative patterns were common on French and Flemish instruments, as can be seen in the plates in this book, though the English makers usually preferred to leave their soundboards plain.

In the case of wind instruments, a wooden tube produces a quite different sound from an ivory tube, and while the ivory may look more beautiful, box-wood sounds much better. Collectors do not change over the centuries, however; even today an eighteenth century flute of ivory will be valued at a far higher figure than a boxwood one. Exotic woods were also used instead of the more ordinary box to enhance the appearance of an instrument. Sometimes such materials were put to a more practical

Plate 51 Pardessus de viole by Paul-François Grosset, Paris, 1742. (*Musikinstrumenten Museum, Berlin, 4220*)

Plate 52 Double-manual
harpsichord by Hieronymus
Hass, Hamburg, 1734. GG–d³,
1 × 16′, 2 × 8′, 1 × 4′, lute
and harp. (*Conservatoire
Museum, Brussels, M.630*)

use; there is a pair of flutes in the Carse Collection at the Horniman Museum (plate IX), made, it is thought, for master and pupil, the one with mounts and key of gold, the other with mounts and key of silver. It was Carse's conjecture that the gold mounted instrument, which is made of satinwood, was for a royal pupil, perhaps Louis XV, and the silver mounted flute, which is of palissander, a wood which was often used in place of box, for his less exalted master. The ivory mounts on the instruments also differ, both in size and in profile, the ferrules on the silver keyed flute being much the larger, suggesting that that instrument was the better of the two; if it were played by the teacher, it would need to have been the better, for he would have been the better judge of a flute. Both have a set of alternative upper-body joints and both fit into the same case, so the differences of woods and of ferrules have the practical purpose of ensuring that there is no confusion about which joint belongs to which flute.

However, many of the world's collections exhibit instruments made with less discretion and with less regard for their ostensible purpose. The more important the collection, the more likely it will be that the most valued instruments will be the most decorative and the least musically useful.

Keyboard Instruments

The Harpsichord

The first half of the eighteenth century was the greatest period of the harpsichord. The English school, with Tabel and his two pupils, Shudi and Kirckman, both of whom outshone him; the German school of Silbermann and Hass; the French of Blanchet and Taskin, all produced the instruments for which Bach, Handel, Couperin and their contemporaries wrote much of their finest music. All three schools of harpsichords differed quite considerably from each other, but all produced instruments of great distinction, with a range of expression, incisiveness and power unknown before or since.

The English harpsichords derived to some extent from the Flemish school of the preceding period, not surprisingly since the first important English makers seem to have been either Flemish immigrants or Flemish trained. The German, as their stringing

(which is described below) would indicate, were more independent; it was only in Germany that a rank of strings at 16′ pitch was at all common, despite which almost all concert harpsichords made in the bad days of the modern revival had such strings. The shape of the case of a north German instrument (plate 52) is quite different from an English or French one. English instruments, so far as their external appearance is concerned, are often beautiful examples of the cabinet maker's art (plate 53), with the entertaining economical fact that the long straight side is often left undecorated with veneer, presumably because it was intended to be placed in a room with that side against the wall. French instruments were often elaborately painted and gilded (plate X) so that externally they share all the characteristics of French furniture. Internally, however, they reflect the enormous esteem in which French harpsichordists held the tone quality of the Flemish instruments of the Ruckers and Couchet dynasty, and many great French makers spent nearly as much time modifying Flemish harpsichords of the previous period, or building new instruments which looked as though they had been so modified and which they could pass off on their customers as being originally by Ruckers, as they did in making instruments wholly of their own.

Such modification was necessary because the music being written by Couperin and his contemporaries all over Europe demanded a wider range than that of the previous generation. As a result, the short octave was filled out and the bass extended where necessary to the low F and extra notes added in the treble. Because of this, the instruments needed to be widened with new or extended wrest planks to hold a greater width of tuning pins, extra wood had to be added to the soundboard on each side, and either new keyboards were fitted into extended keybeds or extra keys made and added. The tail of the instrument often had to be extended, with the addition of new wood to the soundboard at that end, to accommodate the longer bass strings. Such treatment of earlier instruments was called *ravalement* and it included, of course, the alignment and extension of the keyboards of any transposing doubles which had survived without having been altered already. So great was the demand for such ravalé instruments that, as was said in Chapter 1, only two Ruckers harpsichords are known to survive in their original state, and even virginals had their soundboards and roses removed and fitted into new harpsichords, which the purchasers would believe were older instruments that had undergone the ravalement because they bore a rose with Ruckers's initials. Despite such chicanery, the well ravalé French/Flemish harpsichords and the wholly French instruments of this period are such superb instruments that they, or good modern copies of them, are often the preferred instruments of recitalists today.

The standard large harpsichord had two manuals and by the first decade of the eighteenth century the normal range had been extended to five octaves, fully chromatic from top to bottom, although a number of English instruments were made without the lowest accidental, the range being from F upwards without F sharp. With few exceptions the normal disposition was to have two ranks of strings at eight-foot pitch and one at four-foot on the lower manual and to be able to play one of the eight-foot ranks from the upper manual. Some of the north German instruments, such as the one on plate 52, had an additional choir of strings at sixteen-foot

pitch, and occasionally also a choir at two-foot pitch, sounding two octaves higher than one would expect from the key depressed, both also on the lower manual. In addition to these ranks of strings, each of which would differ somewhat in tone quality as well as in pitch, there were various other devices which could produce a difference of sound. These varied from different plucking materials to ways of reducing the vibration of the strings. In France, for example, the *peau de buffle* was introduced in the late eighteenth century, a soft leather to replace the normal quill, which plucked the strings with a more gentle action and so gave a softer sound. Since each choir of strings was plucked with its own row of jacks, one rank of 8' strings fitted with buff leather would sound quite different from another fitted with quill. Another device was the lute stop, very common in England and common also in north Germany, where it was sometimes referred to as the nazard. The lute stop was a separate row of jacks very close to the wrest-plank bridge, which, because they plucked right at the end of the strings, produced a more nasal sound than the normal plucking position. Because this was achieved by an extra row of jacks, it was not

Plate 53 Double-manual harpsichord by Hermann Tabel, London, 1721, no. 43. The only instrument by Tabel known to survive. FF-f³ without FF sharp, 2 × 8', 1 × 4', lute. The jack-rail removed so that the four rows of jacks may be seen. (*Warwickshire Museum Collection, 102/1965*)

necessary to have an extra row of strings for it; either the lute stop jacks or the normally placed jacks on the same set of strings could be used. The harp stop, which was common in France where the lute stop was rare, was a row of soft leather pads mounted on a batten next to the wrest-plank bridge so that, by sliding the batten, the pads could be pushed against the strings to mute them slightly and produce a sound resembling that of a harp.

With all these devices, plus the possibility of coupling both manuals so that all the strings could be played simultaneously from one keyboard, a considerable range of sonorities was available to the harpsichordist. far greater in many ways than that which the pianist can command today. The one thing that the harpsichordist could not do was to move gradually from one sonority to another. He could play at one level and then, by taking his hand from the keyboard and moving a stop lever, change to another, but such change was inevitably sudden and not gradual. In later models he could make such changes by moving a lever with his knee, though the knee levers were not very popular because they were expensive and because players feared that so complex a mechanism would go out of adjustment.

The Pianoforte

Various makers tried to overcome this problem and to produce an instrument which would play both softly and loudly, *piano e forte* in Italian, and move by gradual degrees from the one to the other. The solution that was to be successful in the end, though it made little impact at first, was that of Cristofori who, in about 1700, produced his *gravicembalo col piano e forte*, or harpsichord with soft and loud (plate 54), an instrument that differed from all harpsichords made since the time of Arnault de Zwolle in 1440 in that instead of having jacks with plectra to pluck the strings, it had small hammers, covered with kid leather, to hit them. A pluck consists of pulling at the string with something until the string tension is greater than the rigidity of the plectrum, at which point the plectrum bends and the string leaps past it with a twang, and it is therefore difficult to vary the strength of a pluck; the plectrum can be hard or soft, but the strength of a mechanical pluck cannot be varied from one moment to the next without complicated, and potentially unreliable,

devices. A hammer is quite another matter. Because one is striking the string, instead of moving past it, the string can be struck hard or gently and so produce a sound that is louder or softer, depending entirely on how hard the key which controls the hammer is pressed. The disadvantage of Cristofori's instrument was that, because the instrument was still built as a harpsichord except for the action, the stringing and hammers were light and the sound was, therefore, quiet, much quieter than the contemporary harpsichord, for with light stringing the plucking action is the more efficient. In addition, although it had the advantage of being able to move smoothly from soft to loud within the small range available to it, it had nothing like the range of contrasting sonorities which was available on the harpsichord. The result was that even though people bought examples of the new instrument for the sake of the novelty of its sound, after a while they tired of the lack of contrast, and there are records of a number of Cristofori's instruments in Spain that were converted into harpsichords.

Various makers, the German Silbermann for one,

made examples of the new instrument, but they were not well thought of by established musicians such as J. S. Bach and it was not until the next generation that improved actions, somewhat heavier stringing and above all the new styles of music and the demand for expressive powers, led to the general introduction of the pianoforte and the eclipse of the harpsichord.

The Spinet

A domestic keyboard instrument, if space or cost precluded the use of a harpsichord, was the spinet. This is an instrument which is distinct from the virginals (though it should be remembered that the two names were used interchangeably at all periods) in that, as can be seen in plate 55, the strings run away from the ends of the keys, usually at an angle of about forty-five degrees, instead of being nearly parallel to the line of the front board as on the virginals or running away from the keys in a straight line as on the harpsichord. The jacks of the spinet are set in a straight line, roughly parallel with the front board, whereas those of the virginals (plates V and 13) run diagonally across the soundboard. The virginals is an instrument quite distinct from the harpsichord in shape and in tone quality, but the spinet is essentially a miniature harpsichord even though the shape is somewhat different. The tone of the spinet suffers from the shortness of the bass strings, of course, just as the boudoir grand or the upright piano, which also have short bass strings, can never equal the tone quality of the full-size concert grand.

The spinet was highly popular in England and many survive, a considerable number of them, like that illustrated in plate 55, made by various members of the Hitchcock family, a dynasty that covered a century or so. The spinet was also popular in France, but it seems hardly to have been used in Germany, though the general lack of surviving German keyboard instruments might be because Germany was extensively fought over in the eighteenth century and during the Napoleonic wars, and many instruments may have been destroyed and thus a false impression created. France also, of course, lost a great number of instruments during the Revolution, but in many cases lists were made of what were sold, destroyed or burnt, from which we can gauge the comparative popularity of the spinet. It must be remembered, however, that the popularity of the spinet was based not on its musical capabilities but on its convenience as a domestic instrument and as a substitute for the harpsichord for which there was insufficient money or room.

Travellers' Harpsichords

As with the virginals in the earlier period, small spinets were made for travellers and for others who might wish for a small portable instrument, but because these were small they were always tuned higher than the usual instrument. Since they had even smaller soundboards and even shorter strings than the full-size instruments, their sound was thinner and even less satisfactory to anybody who wished to play at all seriously. A professional musician would have been happy and willing to practise on a clavichord, as has been done at all periods since its invention until well into the nineteenth century (both Mozart and Chopin, for example, carried a clavichord on which to practise during their tours), but an amateur, playing with

Plate 55 Bentside spinet by Thomas Hitchcock, London, no. 1241, c. 1705. GG-g³, 1 × 8'. (*Russell Collection no. 10, Edinburgh University*)

less serious intent but with the desire to hear his or her music as much in its normal tone quality as possible, may well have wanted something nearer to a harpsichord in sound and without the small range and high pitch of the usual travelling spinet. It was presumably for such a clientele that Jean Marius of Paris invented his *clavecin brisé* or broken (collapsible) harpsichord (plate 56). This was a most ingenious device, a single manual harpsichord with the full normal disposition for its period, two 8′ ranks and a 4′, built in three sections. The smallest section, that on the right of plate 56, is designed so that it folds back until it is in line with the middle section, to rest against the longest section on the left with its portion of the keyboard now at the back of the instrument. The next step is to fold the middle and right-hand section right over to rest upside-down on top of the left-hand section, so that the harpsichord is now simply a long box, as wide as it is thick and taking little room as a piece of luggage. Such treatment, of course, did the tuning no good at all and Marius, ever considerate of the convenience of his customers, provided a monochord, a marked scale with a movable bridge under one string, along the left-hand side of the instrument to make tuning quicker and easier, for the player could simply check the pitch of each string against the pitch of the marked points on the monochord. The remains of the monochord can be seen on the instrument illustrated. This particular example of the travelling harpsichord once belonged to Frederick the Great who was an enthusiastic musician and composer.

Marius is also interesting as one of a number of instrument makers who were becoming dissatisfied with the limited abilities of the harpsichord and who were trying to produce instruments with a greater expressive power. His harpsichord with hammers seems not to have attracted much attention, any more than did Cristofori's in his own time, a fate not uncommon among those who try to change the tastes of their time.

The Organ

Undoubtedly the most important keyboard instrument in this period was the organ. Many of the greatest composers were *Kapellmeisters*, directors of music of ecclesiastical establishments, whether for a town, as Bach was at Leipzig, or at a court, as Bach was at Cöthen, and one must remember that a fair number of courts were those of bishops and other Church dignitaries. A glance at Bach's list of works shows that fully half of his compositions were either written for the organ or were choral works for church use, with the organ either as the sole accompaniment or as the mainstay of the continuo, and much the same is true of the majority of his contemporaries. The organ reached its heights in Germany where superb instruments were made, many of which survive to the present day. The organ illustrated on plate 57 is of particular interest since the church to which it belongs, the Wenzelskirche in Naumburg, is one with a long musical tradition. As well as the organ it contained a number of instruments dating from the beginning of the seventeenth century and earlier, many of which are still preserved in the Musikinstrumenten-Museum in Berlin and some of which are illustrated in *The World of Medieval & Renaissance Musical Instruments* (plates 72, 73, 75 in that book), a tradition which did not end, for the trumpet illustrated on plate 47 here also came from the same church and was made by a Naumburg maker.

The organ was built around 1700 and the interior was rebuilt (a common fate for organs, the exteriors of which are often older than the internal pipes and mechanism) around 1745, presumably with the advice of J. S. Bach, for a letter dated 1746 survives, expressing his approbation of the reconstruction;

Plate 56 Clavecin brisé (folding harpsichord) by Jean Marius, Paris, early 18th century. GG/BB-c³, 2 × 8′, 1 × 4′. Originally the property of Frederick the Great. (*Musikinstrumenten Museum, Berlin, 288*)

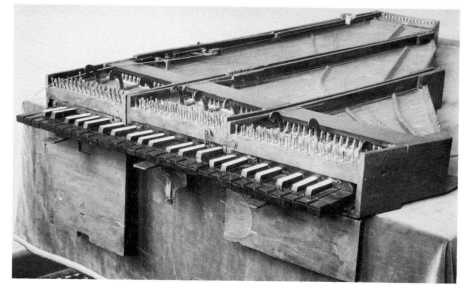

Peter Williams quotes the specification.

In Spain the organs, which were often more elaborate externally than the German though rather simpler internally, had a feature that is always startling to northern European eyes and ears: the trumpets *en chamade* projecting horizontally outwards from the front of the organ (plate 58). When, as often happens in Spanish cathedrals, the organ was split in half with one half on each side of the choir, each with its trumpets projecting out over the choir, both the sight and the sound are stunning in their impact. The appearance of a church organ was always just as important as its sound, and the casework and the visible pipes are designed just as carefully to please and impress the eye as the disposition and the tonal scheme is designed to please the ear, and such considerations are not confined to Spain but apply to the organs of all countries.

The English organs had, as a rule, two manuals or keyboards, very occasionally with an octave of

Plate 58 Organs of Santiago de Compostela Cathedral, 1715, with horizontal trumpets.

pedals. These pedals had no pipes of their own but were simply connected to the keys of the bottom octave of the lower manual with pull-downs as on the Italian positive organ shown on plate 59; thus the bass line could be played on those keys by the feet while the hands were playing other parts elsewhere on the keyboards. Other Italian organs were also comparatively simple instruments.

Throughout the rest of northern and central Europe organs as a rule had three manuals. One controlled a separate small organ behind the organist's back and was therefore called the back-positive (*Rückpositiv* in German); sometimes when it was very small it was all-but under his seat, hence the English chair organ, which, in the course of time, became choir organ. The other manuals controlled the main divisions of the organ, one immediately in front of the organist, the *Brustwerk*, which was sometimes provided with doors that could be closed to produce a more distant sound, and the other, the *Hauptwerk*, containing larger and thus lower pitched pipes. A set of pedals controlled their own pipes, housed in two towers, one on each side of the organ case. Each section of the organ was tonally distinct from

Plate 57 Organ of the Wenzelskirche, Naumburg, by Zacharias Hildebrandt, 1743–46. C–c³. For details of the specification, approved by J. S. Bach, see Williams, *The European Organ*, pp. 157–9.

the others and composers could write organ trios,
with a part for each hand, each on a separate manual,
and a third part for the feet. The French organs were
nearly as elaborate as the German and other northern
European instruments, though their sound was quite
different, as different as Couperin's music is from
Bach's.

As with the harpsichord, the sound of the organ
was terraced; there was an enormous range of
possible sounds, but the organist contrasted one
with another, only changing them when he had the
time to move a hand from the keys for long enough
to change manuals or to push back or draw out a
stop, unless, as sometimes seems to have happened,
he had an assistant to manipulate the draw-knobs
for him. Again as on the harpsichord, the organist
could not get gradually louder or softer until, somewhere around 1700, the swell box, which seems to
have originated in Spain, was introduced. The swell
was a set of doors, which could be opened or closed
by a lever and which allowed the sound of those
pipes that were enclosed in the swell box to escape
more easily and thus more loudly and more loudly
still as the doors were opened wider, and of course
more quietly as they were closed. It would therefore
seem that it was on the organ that the gradual
crescendo and diminuendo were first generally
employed in the early eighteenth century, growing
louder and softer by opening and closing the doors
of the swell, rather than on the pianoforte, which
was invented to produce precisely that effect.
However, although we know that a number of
organs had this device built into them, we do not
know to what extent it was used, for comparatively
little music has indications of the registration, a
recommended list of stops, and even less shows any
change of registration in original manuscripts or
early printed editions. Certainly our normal impression of the music of this period, up to the middle
of the century, is that it was the terraced contrasts
of loud and soft, and more important, of contrasting
but equally loud tone colours, that were normally
conceived by the composers.

The differences between the national schools of
organ building were so great, and the tone colours of
the baroque organ so different from those of the
nineteenth and twentieth centuries, that the differences between eighteenth century and modern per-

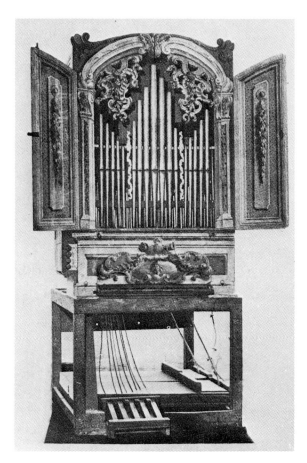

formances of organ music are even greater than those
of orchestral and chamber music. When it is also
remembered that composers rarely gave any indication of registration, one realises that the modern
organist may often be playing the equivalent of a
string trio and making it sound like a symphony
orchestra and, of course, vice versa.

The Clavichord

Organs remained large and expensive instruments.
Even the small positive organ such as that in plate 59,
which could be moved from room to room, was
comparatively expensive and at the same time limited
in expression, for there was usually only a single
manual and, while there was occasionally a pedal at
the front connected with the bellows, it normally
required the cooperation of another person to pump
the bellows and provide the wind for the pipes. As a
result, the organist who wished to practise at home
was under some difficulty. He was under even more

difficulty if he wished to practise in his church, for there he would need light and for a large organ he would quite possibly require a team of blowers to operate the bellows, and all these things cost money; in addition, in the winter he would suffer from the cold. The answer was the clavichord, or often a group of two or even three clavichords such as that in plate 60: two placed on top of each other to represent two of the manuals, for even if his organ had three manuals, the player would not need more than two for practice purposes, and a third fitted with pedals instead of a manual for his feet. With such a combination of clavichords he could, in the warmth and light of his own home, practise everything he might wish or need to play in his church. The only thing that he could not do with such an instrument was to couple the manuals and the pedal together to play on two or all three instruments simultaneously, as he could on his organ, but such a lack was not serious from the practising point of view.

The clavichord was by this time less heavily fretted than it had been in the previous period and the normal arrangement was to have no more than two tangents sharing a pair of strings with some, usually the As and the Ds, having strings to themselves. There was thus still a good deal of economy in the construction, with a number of notes sharing a course with their neighbouring accidental, as on the clavichord in plate 61, for chords which required the simultaneous sounding of two notes a semitone apart were unknown. It was not until the middle of the century that completely fret-free clavichords, with a separate pair of strings for every note throughout the whole compass, became at all common. It is presumably because these were the final instruments made by the greatest makers that they were the ones

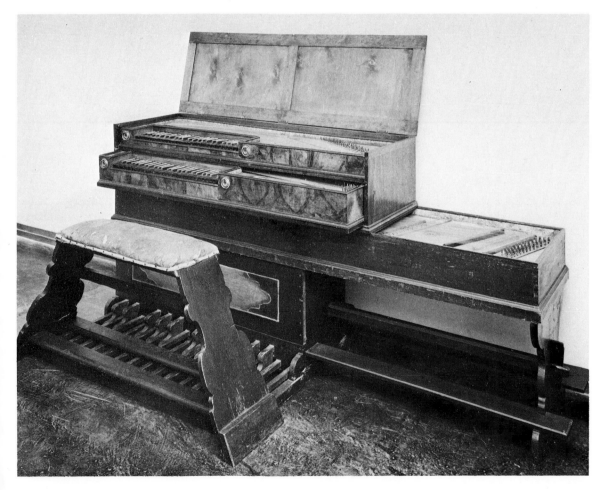

Plate 60 Double-manual clavichord and pedal clavichord by Johann David Gerstenberger, Geringswalde, 1760. Manuals C–d³, fret-free; pedal CC–d with 16′ and 8′. Double-strung throughout. (*Heyer Collection, Musikinstrumenten Museum, Karl-Marx-Universität, Leipzig, 23*)

copied by modern makers at the beginning of the twentieth century revival, and it is only within the past decade or so that makers have begun to recognise the considerable economy of making the lightly fretted instruments of the type played on by the great composers of the baroque era. Not only is it an economy in cost, but it saves the player a good deal of tuning time, for he has only to tune about half the number of strings, the adjacent accidentals being automatically in tune with the note with which they share a pair of strings. Even more important, it is still as true of the clavichords of the early eighteenth century as it was of those of the seventeenth that, because the tension was less than it would be if there were a full complement of strings, the casework can be made lighter and thus more resonant, producing an instrument whose sound, while still far softer than that of any other keyboard instrument, is a great deal louder than those used to normal modern instruments would expect.

The Harp

For concert and professional purposes the harp, the instrument for which Handel wrote his concerto for instance, was still the triple harp (plate 62). A variety of harp introduced in the latter part of the seventeenth century was the hook harp (plate 63), an instrument that had a single choir of strings and hooks set into the neck at the appropriate distance below the tuning pins. When a hook was turned so that it pressed against the string, the sounding length of the string was shortened sufficiently to make it sound a semitone higher than its normal pitch. The hook harp had the disadvantage that a hook could be turned only by a hand which had, perforce, to stop playing for long enough to do so, and then to turn it back when the normal length and pitch were required, so that while one might just have time to turn one hook to raise an F to an F sharp, it would not always be possible to do the same in the next or other octaves, for it would take far longer to

76

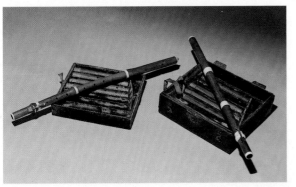

Plate X   Double-manual
harpsichord by Pascal Taskin,
Paris, 1769. FF–f³, 2 × 8′,
1 × 4′ and harp. A fully
developed French harpsichord.
(*Russell Collection no. 15,
Edinburgh University*)

77

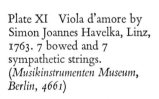

Plate XI   Viola d'amore by
Simon Joannes Havelka, Linz,
1763. 7 bowed and 7
sympathetic strings.
(*Musikinstrumenten Museum,
Berlin, 4661*)

Plate XII   Baryton by Joachim
Tielke, Hamburg, 1686. 6
bowed strings and 25
sympathetic/plucked strings,
the original pegs for which
have been replaced by wrest
pins. Front and back views.
(*Victoria & Albert Museum,
London, 115–1865*)

78

turn the hooks of all the F strings. It was, therefore, a useful instrument for playing in any one key, when it could be preset to the key required, or for playing music which included an occasional accidental, but it could not compare with the triple harp for any elaborate or complex music. It did, however, have the very considerable advantage that it required only one rank of strings, and this not only saved the cost of the other two ranks but also made playing a great deal easier, and makers sought to find a way to produce such an instrument which would be able to play music with more frequent changes of key.

One answer, first tried early in the eighteenth century, was the use of pedals, which were connected to and could turn the hooks, allowing a player to move a hook without taking a hand from the strings. Various models were tried with different numbers of pedals and types of linkage so that one pedal could move all the hooks of the note to which its name was attached (all the F hooks or all the B hooks, for instance). Probably the most successful of these, certainly the one which survives in the greatest number, was that of Nadermann (plate 64) in the middle of the eighteenth century, on which hooks, called *crochets* in French, pulled inwards towards the neck as well as turning, so that they pulled the string against a small bar or nut, thus stopping its length firmly and cleanly at the desired spot. This can be seen more clearly in the detail towards the top of the engraving, which is taken from the illustrations to the section on *Lutherie*, the art of instrument making, from the great *Encyclopédie* compiled by Diderot and D'Alembert. It was this work, more than anything else, which opened the Age of Enlightenment, which brought knowledge of all spheres of activity within the reach at least of all who could read and which opened the doors of learning to all Europe.

Plate 62 Triple harp by John Richards, Llanrwst, 1764. GG-f³ without GG sharp. (*Welsh Folk Museum, St. Fagans, 44.67*)

Plate 63 Hook harp, anonymous. Fully chromatic only in the upper-middle range. (*Welsh Folk Museum, St. Fagans, 45.335*)

79

Plate 64   Single-action pedal
harp by Nadermann, Paris,
mid-18th century. According
to the text from BB flat
upwards, depending on the
number of strings; according
to the plate from C–a³. Fig. 2
(*top right*) shows in detail the
crochet which raises the pitch
by a semitone (*g* in fig. 1);
fig. 3, the retaining pins in the
sound-board; fig. 4, the tuning
pins in the neck (*f* in fig. 1);
fig. 5, the tuning key. (*Denis
Diderot & Jean Lerond
d'Alembert*, Encyclopédie,
Lutherie, *Paris, 1751 and later*)

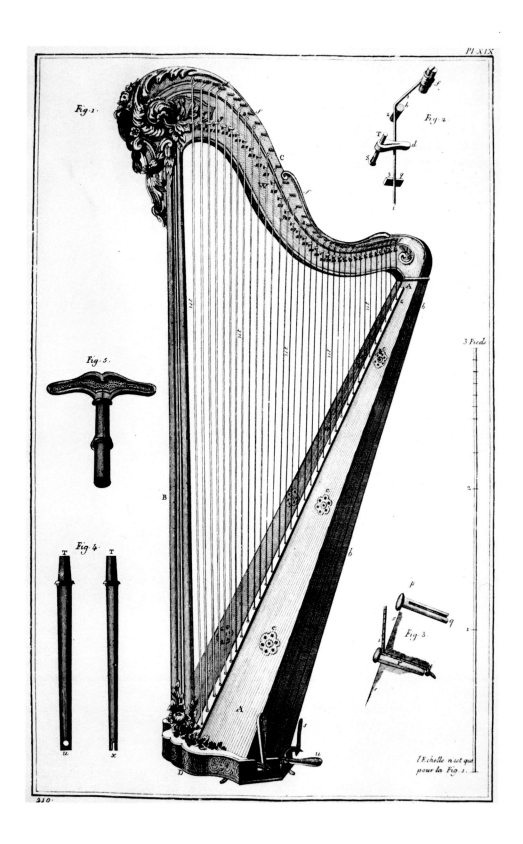

Chapter III
The Classical Era

During the latter part of the eighteenth century considerable changes were made in the use and construction of all instruments, and a number of circumstances both musical and sociological contributed towards these changes. In the middle of the century, the Mannheim school of composers, gathered at a court imbued with a progressive musical spirit and possessing an excellent orchestra, gradually broke away from the baroque concept of music towards a freer and lighter style, aiming always towards a sensuous expressiveness and a rise and fall of dynamic and melody. As the news of what they were doing spread to all the other centres of music in Europe, their contemporaries were most influenced by their use of the expressive crescendo and diminuendo and this, as we shall see, led to both the disappearance of those instruments which proved incapable of such expression and the adoption of new instruments which could carry out this concept, as well as to the gradual modification of all other instruments to enable them better to suit the new music.

The same spirit of unease, of dissatisfaction with the *status quo* and the settled order of things that eventually led to the French and American Revolutions, led composers to question whether music need still be constructed as it had always been, and this was perhaps combined with the feeling that after J. S. Bach there was little further that anyone could go in the baroque style, for among the leaders of the new wave in music were his sons and pupils.

Sociological forces were also at work. Although the orchestra at Mannheim was, like many others, a court orchestra, the spirit of egalitarianism which led to the writings of Thomas Paine and others and to the Revolutions in France and America and to social changes elsewhere that were as great, if less drastically achieved, meant that concerts were no longer reserved to the nobility and the court. The age of large public concerts had begun and music was no longer confined to the drawing room of the palace or the chateau, nor to the small music room

such as that in which Britton had arranged his concerts, but was performed in town assembly rooms and, before long, in purpose-built concert halls. A hall seating an audience of several hundred people, all of whom had paid to hear the music, was very different from a court salon containing the noble family and such members of their entourage as had been invited to attend an evening of polite entertainment in which music was, for many of the listeners, a background noise sufficient to hide the more scandalous portions of their gossip from the ears of their neighbours. Thus in the latter part of the eighteenth century the normal continental circumstances of musical performance reached the same stage that had already been reached in Britain under the Hanoverians. The result was that orchestras quickly became larger. Partly because a greater volume of sound was required for the larger hall and the larger audience, and partly because more wind instruments were introduced at this time, it was necessary that the string instruments should, for the sake of a reasonable balance in the ensemble, in their turn become louder or, if that were impossible, more numerous in order to make more sound.

Thus we have two major influences leading to changes in musical instruments, the one musical and the other sociological. The third great influence was technological, for this was the age of the Industrial Revolution. In the eighteenth century instruments were still made by hand, of course, as the best instruments still are made today; the factories and the assembly lines for musical instruments were a nineteenth century innovation which led to the flood of cheap, partly machine-made instruments which allowed the brass bands of the last century and the school orchestras of the present day to flourish. New materials, however, new techniques and new tools were introduced; for example, all sorts of small parts could often be bought-in, ready made in bulk, to avoid having to waste workshop time on making them. It is apparent, for instance, from work done by Maurice Byrne, that there were specialist makers in London for woodwind keys, and even where a certain instrument maker's style of key is recognisable, he may have had them made for him by a keymaker. Brass tubing was made of thinner brass and of much more precise diameter, which made possible the introduction of tuning slides. Mechanical feeds to lathes and other turning machinery made it cheap and easy to produce covered strings, not only for the bowed and plucked string instruments but also for the keyboards. It was partly this innovation that led to the widespread introduction of the smaller sizes of piano, for without covered strings with overwindings that were both even (so that they did not produce poor tone) and securely laid over the core (so that they would not buzz), such instruments as the square piano could never have had a satisfactory bass.

These three factors—musical, sociological and technological—led to such changes in all musical instruments that within one man's lifetime there was a total and absolute change in the sound of music such as had hardly been experienced in any previous period, nor would be again. There has been no era without change, as has already been apparent in this and in the previous book, and will again be apparent in the next, which will cover the romantic and modern periods, but the changes that occurred in the middle of the eighteenth century were the most radical of all. Not one instrument used by J. S. Bach and his contemporaries survived without considerable alteration, if it survived at all, into the orchestras of Mozart, Haydn and the early Beethoven.

The most fascinating speculation about this period of such rapid and drastic change is: what was it like to live through it? How did Johann Christian Bach and his contemporaries hear their music and what did they think of the changes? After all, J. C. Bach was born in 1735, a year after his father had completed the *Christmas Oratorio* and before he had finished the *Mass in B minor*; he died in 1782, the year in which his erstwhile pupil Mozart wrote *Die Entführung aus dem Serail* and the *Haffner Symphony*. It is hardly possible to imagine a greater musical change in a lifetime, for not only were musical styles changing, as they do with every succeeding generation, but the sonorities, the actual sounds of the music, changed more within his lifetime than in any other, and changed more suddenly.

Musical styles and their accompanying sonorities had slowly built up from the Renaissance, the harmonies and the polyphony of Palestrina unfolding and merging into the summit of that ethos of music, the masterworks of J. S. Bach; and then suddenly there came the total change into the *style galante*, the music that led to Mozart and through him to Beethoven and, until the Viennese revolution of our own century, the music of the present day. We look back at this period of transition with questions and speculation, questions that remain unanswered, speculation that remains unsatisfied, for at the time nobody seems to have noticed any great changes or anything unusual happening at all.

Woodwind Instruments

The Recorder

The desire for expression in music led to the instantaneous extinction of the recorder. As soon as a recorder player blows harder to obtain a louder sound, the pitch of the note goes higher; as soon as he blows more gently to obtain a softer sound, the pitch goes lower. Nor is there much that he can do to compensate for this sharpening and flattening. This is why the organ, which suffers from exactly the same problem, has a reservoir, a set of bellows controlled by springs or weights to maintain a constant pressure, between the main bellows and the pipes; were it not for this reservoir, injudicious pumping would distort the pitch, sharpening as the organ blowers work harder and increase the air pressure and going flat every time they relax their efforts and allow the air pressure to drop. The recorder dropped out of use except in such old-fashioned circles of amateurs of the old music as still existed. The fact that a few recorders made in the second half of the eighteenth century survive suggests that some such circles did exist, but they were of no importance or effect in the main stream of music. The recorder, whose name is said to come from that for a remembrance or a keepsake, was completely forgotten and the word flute came to mean the transverse instrument.

The Flute

Although the transverse flute was similarly affected by stronger or gentler blowing, the player was able to compensate for this and avoid going out of tune. One of the factors controlling the pitch of an instrument is the area of the holes in its body which are open to the ambient air, and the embouchure of the flute, the hole across which the player blows, is as much a hole as any other. If the player rolls the embouchure slightly towards his mouth so that his lower lip covers it a little more, he has reduced the area of open hole and the pitch will be lower. If he rolls the instrument slightly away to uncover the embouchure and move it further away from his lower lip, the area of open hole is increased and the pitch will be higher. Thus he can blow more strongly, so raising the pitch slightly, but simultaneously roll the flute towards his lip and so lower the pitch slightly. If he is sufficiently skilful in combining these procedures, he will be playing at the same pitch the whole time whether he is playing more loudly or more softly. The use of this technique meant that the transverse flute could be played with the expressiveness required in the new style.

In the baroque period composers of orchestral music normally kept to a few well known keys, partly because the keyboard instruments, which were, as we have seen, an essential foundation to the orchestra, were tuned in temperaments which were best adapted to those few keys, and partly because orchestral instruments were happier in their home keys or in those which were close to home. In the classical era the search for a wider field for expression resulted in the use of the less familiar keys, a greater freedom of modulation into other keys during the course of a piece of music, and a more common use of chromatic notes—notes which are not a part of the scale of that key. This had little effect on string instruments, which have always had the ability to play any note within the compass of the fingerboard, though the tuning of the strings of the members of the violin family leads to a general preference for keys with sharps rather than for those with flats. If a certain fingering, a certain spacing of the fingers, is used on the lowest string of the violin, the G string, and then the same fingering is used on the upper strings, F sharps, C sharps, G sharps and so on will automatically be played; in addition, a player is on the whole happier stretching a finger further out, extending it, to sharpen a note than he is when drawing it back, contracting it, to flatten

one, for such contraction tends to cramp the hand. These extra chromatic notes had a much greater impact on the woodwind and, to a lesser extent, due solely to the levels of technology in industry, on the brass. It was during this period that the first fully chromatic brass instruments, the Amorschall and the key trumpet, were invented and that playing techniques which permitted chromaticisms such as hand-stopping were introduced; to these we shall return in due course.

On the woodwind the principal effect was the introduction of new keywork to cover additional finger holes. We have seen that the flute, like the oboe, was provided with a key for the lowest chromatic note (plate 65, top), a note which cannot be cross-fingered. In the baroque period chromatic notes were usually only passing notes on which it was not too serious if the tone were weaker than the natural notes of the scale—this weakness is almost inevitable if lower finger holes, which should be venting the note clearly, are to be closed to flatten the pitch as is done in cross-fingering. As the chromatic notes became more important to the structure of the melody and also more frequently used, this weakness became unacceptable and the players required a greater facility in playing such notes if only because of their greater frequency. The result was that further keys were fitted on the flute for F natural (right ring finger), G sharp (left little finger) and B flat (left thumb). These, with the existing D

Plate 65 FLUTES. *Top to bottom:* 1 key flute by Phipps & Co, London (II 4); 4 key flute marked, but probably not made by, Drouet, London (II 6); 6 key flute by Richard Potter, London (II 8); lower body-joint and foot descending only to C sharp, by Potter (I 30); 5 key flute with upper C natural key by William Milhouse, London (IV 130); 8 key flute by Potter with tuning slide drawn and foot keys removed (IV 200). All late 18th century except the 'Drouet', which is probably *c.* 1820. (*Author's Collection*)

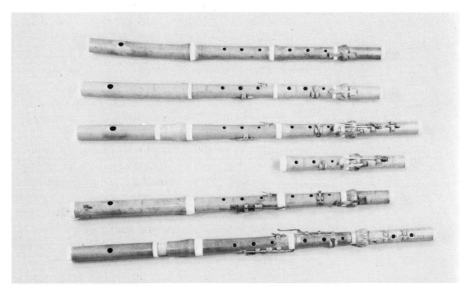

sharp key, made up the four-key flute, the second one down on plate 65, which became the standard instrument at the beginning of the second half of the eighteenth century. Conservative players kept to the old one-key flute throughout the century, and indeed it was possible to buy one-key flutes into the early years of the twentieth century.

At much the same time the range of the flute was extended. The lowest note had been D, a tone above middle C, and now the foot was made long enough to carry two open-standing keys, the first to produce C sharp when it was closed and the second to sound middle C (plate 65, third flute down). When it was first introduced this extension was, as is usual with such developments, attacked by the established players such as Quantz who considered that it ruined the tone of the instrument, and even today these two keys at the bottom end of the instrument appear to be extras. Just when the C foot became generally adopted is still unknown, but it was probably around or not long after 1760 or 1770. There are a few instruments of the same period which, like the flute that Quantz tried and condemned, have half the extension, with only the C sharp key, and the lower-body joint and foot of such an instrument can be seen in plate 65 below the six-key flute; we know nothing of their use. Certainly the C foot was known to Mozart who used it in a number of his works.

During the latter part of the century two further keys were adopted. One was for the upper C natural (plate 65, fourth flute down) and the other the long F natural key (plate 65, bottom) so that this most common of accidentals could be taken with either the right ring finger or the left little finger. On most flutes, as on the one in the plate, the long F key was an extra key running down the far side of the instrument to its own hole opposite that of the short F key. Some makers adopted the ingenious expedient of fitting an additional lever to lift the pad of the key already provided, thus obviating the need to drill another hole and avoiding the resulting extra chamber in the bore, for when closed every finger hole creates a chamber in the bore which may have an adverse effect on tone and intonation. With these keys, the eight-key flute was established, and this was the normal instrument for the last part of the century and remained in common use right through the nineteenth century.

Various materials were used for key-pads, the commonest on the early instruments being a square of kid leather. In 1785 Richard Potter, the maker of the six-key and the eight-key flutes in plate 65 and of the lower-body joint and C sharp foot, took out a patent covering a number of inventions, one of which was for the keys with pewter plugs that can be seen in the plate. The holes were often bushed with a brass tube to give these plugs a firm seating, and the foot keys have been removed from the eight-key flute so that these can be seen. Potter's patent pewter plugs remained in use by many makers for the C and C sharp keys of the foot joint well into the middle of the nineteenth century, probably because, as Philip Bate suggests, this material kept its shape better than others when it was not in contact with the seating of its hole, and these were open-standing keys which were only in contact with their seating when those notes were played.

Other alterations in the flute included a slightly greater expansion of the bore in the foot joint, so that the open end of the instrument was almost the same diameter as the top of the lower-body joint; thus the flute contracted in bore from that point over a distance of about fifteen centimetres and then expanded to the same diameter over a distance of only about six centimetres. This helped to increase the volume of sound that could be produced, as did an increase in the size of the embouchure, which became larger and more oval; this had the added advantage that there was a greater area available to help control the tuning of the instrument. Another change was the general adoption of the tuning slide in place of separate upper-body joints for different pitches. This was aided by the invention of the movable cork; a greater or shorter length of flute should, if the instrument is to be well in tune, be reflected in a greater or lesser distance from the cork which closes the head to the embouchure. Corks were provided with a screw which passed through the end-cap (the end of this screw can be seen projecting from the end-cap of the lowest flute but one on plate 65) and by turning the cap the screw could be drawn out or pushed in, thus moving the cork. One of the features of Potter's 1785 patent was for a screw marked with lines, as were the tenons between the joints; the player was supposed to ensure that each tenon and the screw were set to the same line.

Peripatetic Instruments

It is the fashion today to disapprove of those who go on picnics and walks armed with their transistor radios, but this is only the current expression of an unceasing stream of peripatetic music. In the 1920s it was portable gramophones and in the 1880s ukuleles and banjos. Previously the popular instrument for such diversions had been the musical walking stick in a number of forms including, in the early nineteenth century, almost every instrument then in use. What seems to have been the earliest and was certainly the most commonly seen in the late eighteenth century, was the walking stick flute (plate 66). It was a part of the spirit of the age that when a young lady saw a beautiful view she would be expected to immortalise it in water colours; a gentleman would be more often expected to salute it with a flow of appropriate melody, and hence the musical walking stick, as suited to its times as the pocket mouth-organ a few years ago and the 'tranny' today.

The Oboe

Oboe makers, especially in France, had continued to refine the oboe, to produce an instrument ever more flexible in dynamic and sweet in tone. English makers, on the other hand, had preferred the more robust sound of the early eighteenth century instrument and had made little change until, under the same influences that affected all the other instruments, the old English oboe was swept away and the newer French oboe imported and copied in England. The bore was narrower and the reed longer and narrower, the tone as a result being sweeter and more piercing, fully able to stand up to the rest of the orchestra, whereas the older English instrument had been sufficiently soft that Handel had at times used as many oboes in his orchestra as he had violins. No longer was this necessary; the new oboe was used one to a part, as the modern instrument is today.

Around the middle of the eighteenth century the oboe was unique among woodwind in that it lost a key (plate 67). This was not because of any greater simplicity in its music but only because it was in this period that makers accepted the fact that players had decided to play all the woodwind with the left hand above the right. Whereas in the earlier periods it had been necessary to accommodate left-handed players with a duplicated E flat key, this was now agreed to be unnecessary. It seems probable that it was the adoption of the C sharp key on the clarinet that settled the question of which hand should be uppermost, for as soon as this second long key for the little finger of the upper hand, running down to the foot of the instrument, was adopted, a firm decision had to be made. It would be impossible to make these long keys accessible to either hand or to duplicate them and players had to make up their minds to agree on a uniform practice. Also, of course, the new keys for the flute could be reached only one way round, and again a decision was necessary. It would appear from pictures that in the earlier periods more players kept the left hand above than the right and that practice became universal. In fact, although one speaks of right-handed and left-handed in this regard, there is nothing particularly left- or right-handed about either position save that the flute must be held out to one side or the other. So it was that the left-hand hole on the oboe for the E flat was no longer drilled and the key no longer fitted. However, instrument makers tend to be conservative and for many years thereafter the long open-standing C key was still made with a fish-tail touch, as can be seen in plate 67, just as though a player might wish to take it with the left little finger.

Chromatic keys were introduced on the oboe more slowly than on the other woodwind instruments since, partly because of its narrow bore and partly because of its narrow double reed, which is well under the control of the player, the oboe is much more responsive to cross-fingerings and similar techniques. Since it was comparatively easy to produce chromatic notes without the use of extra keys, there was little point in adding to the weight and to the cost of the instrument, and in adding to the worries of the player and to the technical demands made upon him, by fitting unnecessary keys. As a result, the two-key oboe was in regular use into the early years of the nineteenth century and oboes with a greater number of keys were much less common than flutes and other instruments.

Two instruments which did not survive the change

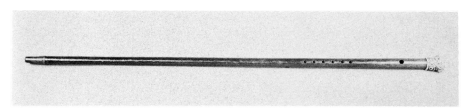

Plate 66 Walking stick piccolo, anonymous, c. 1800. (*Author's Collection, VI 140*)

Plate 67 Two-key oboe by Henry Kusder, London, late 18th century. (*Bate Collection, 23, Oxford University*)

of musical style were the oboe d'amore and the oboe da caccia; the cor anglais or English horn (neither a horn nor particularly English), which can be seen on plate 68, was the only large oboe to survive and it appears only very occasionally—for instance in Haydn's Symphony No. 22—and it was not really accepted even as an occasional member of the orchestra until the middle of the nineteenth century. There were probably two reasons for the demise of the larger oboes. One was that the concept of the homogeneous reed-band had died out. The other, and more important, was that a new instrument had become accepted and established. This instrument, which was easier to play, required only a single reed, which was cheaper, and, because it was backed by a solid mouthpiece, was less prone to accidental breakage than the double reed. Above all, it had not only as great a range on one instrument as the whole family of oboes had on three sizes of instrument, but it had an infinitely greater range of expression throughout that range. This was, of course, the clarinet.

One larger oboe did survive in England and its use is sufficiently mysterious to merit discussion. This was the tenner hoboy or vox humana, a number of which are preserved in collections and which resemble no other instruments of their family. The normal oboe of this period was a fairly ornate instrument with a bulb here, a boss there and some neat turning elsewhere. Even the simple, straight-topped English oboes were obviously well made and elegant instruments, and sometimes, as on the one illustrated in plate 67, they had ivory finials and ferrules. The English tenor oboe, on the other hand, including those made by the best makers such as Stanesby and Collier, was an uncompromisingly plain and undecorated wooden tube, with no pretensions to elegance, as can be seen on plate 69. While the instrument is in unison with the cor anglais and the earlier tenor oboe, taille and oboe da caccia, it is quite different from all these in shape and in

sound, and nothing seems to be known of its use. One might guess that some military or other bands kept to the old idea of the reed band and that these **very** plain instruments were made for that purpose, but since the treble part would have been played on **an** ordinary oboe and the bass presumably on a bassoon, also of normal construction, why not use a cor anglais for the tenor? Or, if the bulbous bell of the cor anglais sufficiently altered the tone to make it unsuitable for such use, retain the open bell of the older tenor oboe or the flared bell of the oboe da caccia? Obviously the straight body of the vox humana is easier to make, and thus cheaper, than the curved body of the cor anglais, but this still does not explain the extreme simplicity, so simple as to appear almost crude, of the vox humana. The English tenor oboe remains a mystery.

The Clarinet

The clarinet did not become at all generally available until well into the second half of the eighteenth century. Authors such as Rendall and Baines have listed works for the instrument from the first half of the century but when these are compared with the works surviving for other instruments, or set against the lists of all known works by their composers, it is clear that the clarinet was still an unusual instrument for which it was interesting to write an occasional piece but that it was not regarded as a serious or regular member of the orchestra. This attitude continued for an extraordinarily long time. To take one example only, when Haydn was writing the second set of his London symphonies in the 1790s, he was quite clearly approaching this new instrument, which he must have heard on his first visit to London, with extreme caution. Even Mozart, who wrote for the clarinet with the utmost fluency when he was composing solo works for his friend Anton Stadler, wrote for it as an orchestral instrument only in his last few works, though he obviously appreciated its qualities and its abilities much more clearly than Haydn.

A vicious circle operates with musical instruments just as with many other objects. If there are no players of a new instrument in a certain city, none of the composers who are writing music for the orchestras in that area include it in their scores; if there is no music being written for the instrument, there is no inducement for any local players to take up the new instrument, nor for established players of it to move into the area. If there is a demand for the performance of music from elsewhere which includes parts for that instrument, there are two options open: to import a player who does play the instrument, or to reorchestrate the music so that it can be played without that instrument. Throughout most of the eighteenth century, and later, the latter solution was adopted as a matter of course. Sometimes when a composer had used a certain orchestration in a work that was later performed in another city where additional instruments were available, he would re-score it. Mozart's Symphony No. 40 in G minor is a case in point; it was originally written without clarinets and Mozart later constructed two clarinet parts, mainly by taking bits out of the oboe parts and by some doubling-up, but with a little new music here and there. From the middle of the nineteenth century onwards, music was written for symphony orchestras, usually for the international market, and it was up to the orchestra that wished to play the work to make sure that it had access to any odd instruments that might be required. Before then, and certainly before Beethoven's days, music was almost invariably written for a particular orchestra, and the composer would know what instruments were available and how many of them there were in that orchestra; he would also usually know how competent all the individual players were and would write accordingly. And thus, to return to the clarinet, it was only in a few cities and courts such as Mannheim where there were clarinets and clarinettists available that composers regularly included them in their scores.

As the clarinet became better known it became ever more popular, for its range, its beauty of tone and its expressive power were greater than those of

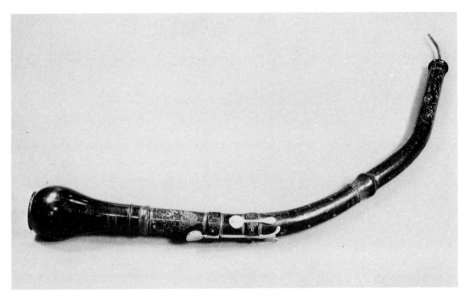

Plate 68   Cor anglais by Gaetano Bimboni, Florence, *c.* 1780. Two keys. (*A. C. Baines, on loan to Bate Collection, x24, Oxford University*)

any other instrument. It acquired two extra keys, first the same E flat key as on the flute and oboe (plate 70, right) and then a long C sharp key, which, with the earlier long B natural key, ran up the side of the tube for the upper (now always the left) little finger. Such five-key clarinets (plate 70, middle and left) survive in tolerable quantities in collections and, with the six-key clarinet which on the Continent had a G sharp key and in England a trill key instead, these were the standard late eighteenth century forms of the instrument. It would seem that this was the maximum number of keys that players were willing to tolerate.

Like the flute, the clarinet suffered from a reluctance to respond to cross-fingering in order to produce the sharps and flats of keys distant from its basic scale, but instead of fitting yet more keys, as on the flute, the solution adopted was to provide extra instruments. A clarinet in B flat (plate 70, middle) would be used for music in that key, in F and in

Plate 69   Vox humana (tenor oboe) by Cahusac, London, second half 18th century. Two keys. (*Victoria & Albert Museum, London, 297–1882*)

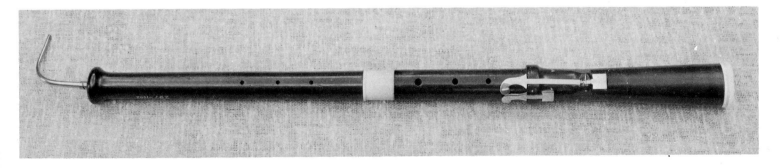

flatter keys. A clarinet in C (plate 70, left and right) was used in that key and perhaps for F and for G. For music in the key of D and in A and in other sharper keys, players would use either an A clarinet or a longer middle joint to convert the B flat clarinet into an A clarinet. There were other sizes too, but the smaller instruments in higher pitches (the highest then normally available seems to have been the F a fifth above the usual B flat clarinet) were so different in tone that they were less often used orchestrally, just as those below the A were also regarded as special instruments, the G clarinet being sometimes known as the *clarinette d'amour* and often being provided with the bulb bell, in German *Liebesfuss*, or love foot, because it was used on the d'amore instruments. The clarinet in F was rare (except in a special form to which we shall return in a moment), and that in E flat was also either rare or a military instrument. Below that pitch, the bass clarinet in B flat, an octave below the normal instrument, was already occasionally in use.

The special form of the F instrument was the basset horn (plate 71), an instrument which, like so many, is of unknown or speculative origin. It is generally thought to have been invented by Mayrhofer in the second half of the century; the existence of the fabulous Herr Horn is now discounted by most authorities. What distinguishes the basset horn from all other clarinets is its range. The clarinet is a transposing instrument; that is to say, the player reads one set of notes but the sounds that result are at different pitches from those that he reads, the actual pitch depending upon the length of the instrument. This is to make it easier to play on a range of instruments of the same type. If the player is to put down one size of clarinet and pick up another it would make his life unnecessarily complicated if, when he saw the note middle C for example, he had to put his hands into a different position on the new instrument from when he played middle C on the other instrument. The obvious solution is for the written middle C to require the same position of the hands on whichever instrument he is playing and for the size of the instrument to determine the pitch of the note that he sounds. The music that he plays from is, of course, written so that the notes that are sounded fit the music played by the rest of the orchestra. On all the clarinets save for the basset

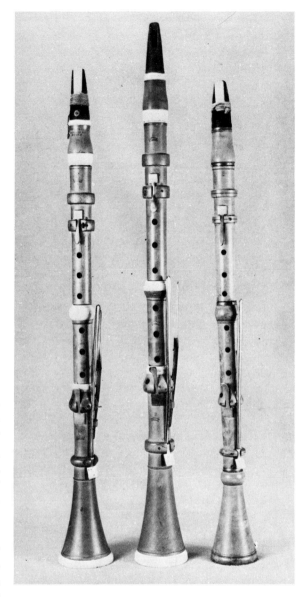

horn, the lowest note that can be written for them is the E below middle C (a few modern instruments have an E flat to avoid the need for a separate A clarinet). On the C clarinet, when the player reads the low E, that is the note which will be produced; on the B flat it will sound a whole tone lower, on the A a semitone lower still; on the D clarinet, on the other hand, it will sound a whole tone higher than written, and so on. Only the basset horn had an extension so that it could play down to its written low C, sounding the F immediately below the bass stave. This was made possible by an extension which was sometimes known as the book: a block of wood which looked like a book in shape and which accommodated three lengths of tubing drilled in the wood so that the tube first went down the book, continuing straight on from the main tubing of the instrument, then turned up again through a U-bend, and then turned down again through another U-bend and passed out of the book into the bell, which was usually of brass. Because the diameter of the bore was very little wider than that of the B flat instrument, whereas the length of the tubing was much greater, the tone was quite different from that of the normal instrument, having a reedy solemnity which Mozart, for one, found attractive and particularly suitable for his Masonic music and especially for music of mourning.

In recent years, detailed study of Mozart's Clarinet Concerto has revealed that some of the lines in the lower part of the range are broken in odd ways. It appears as though the figuration was originally written for an instrument with an unusually low compass but has subsequently been arranged for a shorter instrument. Analysis has suggested that an extra third in the bass, taking the compass down to the written low C instead of to the E, would smooth out these oddities and would allow all the figuration to fall into logical shape. On the strength of this and because Anton Stadler, for whom the work was written, is known to have had such an instrument, a number of players have had basset clarinets in A made on which the music can be played as it is thought to have been written. It is, of course, the dream of all those working in this field that one day the autograph might be found, which would eliminate any uncertainty, and that perhaps a late eighteenth century basset clarinet might turn up. Since, however, it seems probable that Stadler was the only player who had such an instrument, the chances of this happening are slender. If he were the only clarinettist so equipped, this would at least explain why all the printed editions of the concerto, even the oldest, have these modifications that allow the work to be played on a normal clarinet.

The Bassoon

The bassoon showed rather fewer changes in this period than some of the other woodwind instruments. This is because, like the oboe, it is a comparatively narrow bored instrument played with a double reed and is thus more responsive than the flute or the clarinet to cross-fingering, needing less help from extra keys to obtain chromatic notes. Even today the bassoon has the least regard of all woodwind instruments for the 'official' fingerings and, especially in the upper part of its compass, every player has to experiment with fingerings until he finds those which best suit his type of reed, his style of playing and the instrument he is using. The bassoon is so responsive to its own and to its player's idiosyncrasies that the average eighteenth century player's response to any suggested improvements may well have been the decision to leave well alone. The four-key bassoon remained the normal instrument well into the latter half of the century, but by the last quarter of the century the six-key bassoon, with two extra keys for E flat and F sharp, had been introduced. This can be seen on plate 72, which shows two instruments, that on the left from the finger side and that on the right from the thumb side, and it remained the normal pattern of bassoon which lasted into the nineteenth century. The three-key bassoon (plate 32) was the standard instrument from its introduction in the latter part of the seventeenth century until well into the eighteenth century, the four-key bassoon (plate 33, left) from somewhere around 1720 for about fifty years, and then the six-key instrument (plate 72) for most of another half century.

Over this period the external shape of the instrument changed somewhat, as can be seen by comparing plates 32, 33 and 72, but this was partly due to changing styles in wood-turning, especially once it had become customary to fit the wing joint close against the long joint. The bore shows some regional variation, with English instruments often having much wider crooks than their continental contemporaries. The major change in the middle of the eighteenth century was to the bore of the bell joint. Early eighteenth century bassoons almost invariably have a considerable choke in the bore of the bell. The diameter of the bore expanded slowly but steadily from the tip of the crook, where the reed is fitted, to the top of the long joint; it then contracted sharply to a point about two-thirds of the way up the bell, where the diameter was not much greater

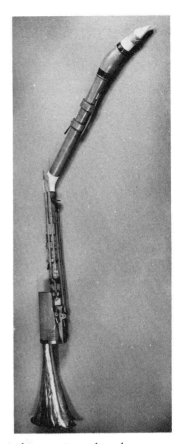

Plate 71 Basset horn by Heinrich Grenser, Dresden, *c.* 1790. 6 keys and 2 basset keys. (*Bate Collection, 489, Oxford University*)

Plate 72 · BASSOONS. *Left:* by Henry Kusder, London, with keys by John Hale, showing the finger side (33); *right:* by William Milhouse, Newark, showing the thumb side (34). Both with six keys, second half 18th century. (*Bate Collection, Oxford University*)

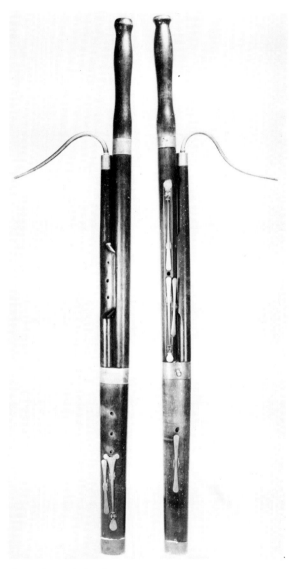

than that of the bottom of the long joint; it then usually expanded again very slightly to the open end. This presumably served the double function of avoiding too open or raucous a tone and of controlling the tuning of some of the notes. In the latter part of the eighteenth century, this constriction of the bell was opened out, being replaced eventually by a continuation of the expansion of the rest of the bore, though there are some instruments which seem to have an almost cylindrical bell joint. This opening of the bell increased the volume produced, with a somewhat more open tone quality, and alterations in tuning could be compensated for by different cross-fingerings or by control of the reed.

It may have been this more open tone quality and the lack of skill of some players in controlling the tuning, which led to occasional contemporary comparisons of the bassoonist with an old goat and other even less flattering remarks, but these were usually made about bad amateur players. There are many far more complimentary references to professional players, and the way in which Haydn treated the bassoon, as a soloist playing in octaves or even in unison with the first violins, indicates that its sound was greatly prized. The bassoon was one of the leading instruments throughout the eighteenth century, for it was the wind bass of the first part of the century, often playing alone with the chordal continuo instruments when accompanying other wind instruments, and playing with the bowed string bass instruments, the cello and double bass, when everybody was playing in the tuttis. It retained its function as a wind bass in the latter part of the century and also frequently shone out as a tenor soloist. As well as being used in the orchestra, it was the normal bass of the military band and of the bandstand combination of two oboes, two horns and one or two bassoons, to which two clarinets were often added and for which so many composers wrote serenades and divertimenti. Such combinations seem to have been commonly employed both out of doors and indoors in the latter part of the eighteenth century and the early nineteenth century and not only is there a good deal of original music for them, but all the popular operas of the day were arranged for them. Most of the arrangements for wind octet of Mozart's operas and Beethoven's *Fidelio* survive and have been printed in modern editions, and more are being discovered all the time, including a number of Rossini's operas.

A further function of the bassoon, particularly in England, was as the bass of the church band. Comparatively few churches, especially in the villages, possessed an organ, for even where a church had once been wealthy enough to have such an instrument many had been destroyed by the Puritans during the Civil War and under the Commonwealth and never replaced. While the Commonwealth lasted church music was usually simple enough that it could be sung unaccompanied, and even the very basic four-part settings of Tate and Brady in the latter part of the seventeenth century were designed for unaccompanied voices. But as more elaborate music made its way into church services, the community would need either to face the expense of an organ or to find some other means of supporting the voices. A common solution was the church band, a heterogeneous combination of whatever instruments could be found and of whoever in the village could play them. One of the most frequently used instruments was the bassoon, and it was one of the most useful. It could provide a solid bass, it could sing out a tenor part and its tone was so clear and penetrating that it would seldom be drowned however strong the voices might be. It was sufficiently solid to withstand a good deal of knocking about and its reed, despite its fragile appearance, would put up with an amazing amount of abuse before it refused to function.

It was as much because of the reed as anything else that the clarinet was far more often used than the oboe in such bands by the end of the century. The oboe reed, like that of the bassoon, is made of two thin blades of cane, carefully shaped, gouged and scraped, and then tied together and lapped with waxed thread to prevent air escaping through the edges, but the oboe reed is long, very thin and extremely delicate, and is ruined by the slightest knock. The clarinet reed, on the other hand, is a single blade of cane and is flat on the underside instead of having to be gouged to a rounded profile. Although it too is delicate and fairly easily spoiled, it will stand up to rather more abuse than the oboe reed and it has the great advantage that when in use it is supported by the mouthpiece of the instrument. The bassoon reed is just as difficult to make initially as the oboe reed and is about the same length; however, it is considerably wider as well as thicker and is thus better able to stand being dropped or leant against a pew. In addition and perhaps more important, it seems to continue to function, at least in the lower part of the register, which is all that matters for such use, with cracks in it and chips out of it long after any other sort of reed would have had to be thrown away. As a result, the bassoon was far better able to withstand the vicissitudes of casual use than either the oboe or the clarinet.

There is still comparatively little known of the effect of the materials of which woodwind instruments are made on their tone quality. Certainly most players are convinced that the materials, the boxwood of the oboes, flutes and clarinets, and the light maple of the bassoons of this period, are the main reason why the eighteenth century instruments sound so much sweeter than the modern ones, but in their present state of knowledge, most acousticians would deny that this has a bearing on the sound. There are other factors, of course: reeds differ and the number of holes differ. The holes have two effects: one, which has already been mentioned, is that the creation of cavities or chambers in the bore of the instrument affects the vibration of the air column; the other is that the more holes that are open, the more clearly a note is vented and thus the louder, and perhaps the harder, its sound will be. Also, any cross-fingering will mute the tone slightly, again in contrast to the more open sound of the modern instrument, while one effect of modern keywork is to add weight to the instrument itself and inhibit its vibration. In sum, we know little of the reasons for the differences in tone quality, but anyone who hears the woodwind instruments of the classical period will be immediately aware that the differences exist and that modern instruments have no way of imitating those of earlier periods.

Brass Instruments

The most obvious change in the use of trumpets and horns in the middle of the eighteenth century is that they were expected to be able to play in many more keys than had previously been the custom; this was made possible by much greater use of the crook. In the baroque period it was normal to have two or three trumpets, one for each key in which trumpets were normally used, and for horns to have only a small number of crooks, but from the middle of the century onwards both horns and trumpets were built to suit the highest normal key and the instrument was lengthened to put it into other keys by inserting various lengths of additional tubing between the mouthpiece and the instrument. These additional lengths have three names in English, depending upon their size and shape. Very short lengths, an inch or two long, are called bits or tuning bits; these were common in the baroque and early classical periods, before tuning slides were used, since they were the only way of adjusting tuning.

Longer but still straight lengths of tubing, sufficiently long to change the pitch by a semitone or a whole tone, depending upon the full length of the instrument, are called shanks. Longer pieces of tubing that are bent or coiled into loops are called crooks. By the end of the century a French horn would have been provided with a set of nearly a dozen crooks, for B flat alto, A, G, F, E, E flat, D, C, B natural basso and B flat basso. In addition to these, some horns had rarer crooks such as that for F sharp; the only work played today for horns in that key is Haydn's Symphony No. 45, *The Farewell*. Expense was sometimes saved by using couplers with the C crook for the low B and B flat, a survival of the older system of one or two master crooks and a few couplers, the loops of cylindrical tubing which fit between the crook and the instrument and which can be seen in plates 37 and 75. In central and eastern Europe an extra shank for C alto was almost always included, but this is very seldom found with horns in Britain or France; it is a crooking that was frequently used by Haydn while he was at Esterháza and by his contemporaries and which produces a beautiful clear, high sound, but it was not usually demanded by composers in western Europe. Trumpets were similarly provided with tuning bits and a pig-tail crook for D, the mouthpiece going straight into the instrument for E flat, and a crook for C and either a longer crook or a coupler for B flat an octave lower than the modern trumpet.

The Horn

By far the most important change in the horn at this period was in playing technique. It was discovered, and the discovery is always credited to the Bohemian virtuoso at the Dresden Court, Anton Hampl, that placing the hand in the bell modified the sound in two ways. One was to quieten it, and it appears that it was while endeavouring to produce a quieter sound by holding a handful of cloth in the bell that Hampl discovered these effects. Once the sound could be made quieter and the somewhat raucous edge to the tone moderated, the horn became a far more acceptable member of the orchestra than it had been in the previous period, and indeed it became the only brass instrument commonly employed. Far more music was written in the rest of the eighteenth century for an orchestra of strings and woodwind and a pair of horns than for orchestras with horns, trumpets and timpani, possibly because of remaining traces of the guild restrictions on the use of trumpets and drums but more probably because the new sound of the horn blended so beautifully with the woodwind and the strings. The other effect of the hand in the bell was of great importance to soloists, though it had rather less impact on the normal orchestral players. This was that the pitch was flattened and that the extent of the flattening could be controlled by the amount that the bell was occluded. By using this technique, it became possible to play all the notes of the diatonic scale from the G below the treble stave (the third harmonic) to the C above the stave (the sixteenth harmonic) and, with more skill and some loss of tone at the bottom of this range, the chromatic notes as well. Below the low G, the horn is sufficiently flexible to allow the player to lip most notes by the process known to players as lip-faking and to scientists as factitious notes, a process that allowed Beethoven to write the pedal G between the first and second harmonics (the $1\frac{1}{2}$ harmonic) and Schubert to write the low E (the $2\frac{1}{2}$ harmonic), and that Haydn often entertained himself, his second horn and his audience by using. Above the top C, the harmonics are a semitone or less apart, as can be seen in figure 2 on page 56, and are, anyway, seldom required. The main use of this discovery was that it allowed the horn to become a fully melodic instrument in the middle part of the range, where playing is the least strain and the least effort; in the previous generation, on the other hand, when only the natural harmonics were employed with a little bending by the lip, melodic parts could be written from only the eighth harmonic upwards.

The one disadvantage of this process was that the hand-stopped notes, those for which the hand closed or partly closed the bell, were very different in tone quality from those notes played with an open bell. It became a matter of pride among players to minimise and indeed to eradicate this difference of tone quality. The hand was positioned so that there would be as little difference as possible between the sounds of the natural harmonics, the so-called open notes, and those of the hand-stopped notes, and this was achieved by stopping all notes to a lesser or greater degree. The result, of course, was that the sound produced by a solo horn player was softer than that of either the earlier or the later instrument, so much so that Mozart could write a quintet for horn, violin, two violas and cello and have no fears about the balance, and Brahms in the following century could write a trio for horn, violin and piano in which the only fear might be that the violin and the piano would drown the sound of the horn. Today, however, now that valves are used and players have drawn their hands much further out of the bell, the horn is more likely to drown the other players.

Orchestral players made less use of the hand-stopping technique. On the whole, parts were restricted to the harmonic series, but composers grew much freer in their use of such harmonics as the F on the top line of the treble stave (the eleventh harmonic), which is, in fact, almost exactly halfway between F and F sharp. The player would be expected to stop down for F and either to open up the eleventh harmonic for F sharp or more likely, since it works better on most instruments, to stop down from the twelfth harmonic. As a result, when a composer wrote either F or F sharp with a sforzando, demanding a sharp attack, he expected to hear a brassy sound, usually indicated today as a special effect by writing a little cross over the note; it is one of the ironies of the modern mechanised instrument that tonal effects of this sort, carefully built into the sound of the orchestra by the composer, are absent today because they do not happen if the player uses his valves instead of his hand. Whether orchestral players in the latter part of the eighteenth century were hand-stopping or not, they followed what had now become normal practice by keeping the hand in the bell to moderate the sound and to improve the tuning of any poor notes, which can be done with slight movements of the hand.

Also introduced in this period was the tuning slide: a section of tubing fitting telescopically into the main body of the tube (plate 73). Such telescopic tubing had, of course, been common on the trombone and the draw trumpet in the late Middle Ages, but there is a considerable technological difference between tubing that can be moved freely to obtain different notes and tubing that fits so closely that it will maintain its position without the player having to hold it but which can be moved easily when necessary. It was only with the greatly increased precision with which tubing of thin metal could be

Plate 73 Inventions Horn (hand horn with tuning slide) with some of its set of crooks, by Courtois aîné, Paris, end of the 18th century. (*Musikinstrumenten Museum, Berlin, 3021*)

drawn or rolled up from sheet that it became possible to produce a tuning slide such as we are accustomed to today. The tuning slide met with some opposition because it meant introducing some cylindrical tubing into the horn, which had been conical in bore. However, the couplers which had been used in the past were cylindrical, so this objection was easily overcome. The tuning bits, which had been previously the only way of making slight alterations in the length of the tubing, tended to wobble and upset the player's embouchure, since they were narrow in bore in order to fit between the mouthpiece and the top of the crook. The new tuning slide was welcomed because its adoption meant that tuning bits could be abandoned; the horn equipped with such a slide was called an *Inventions Horn*.

With the acceptance of the Inventions Horn, it became possible to use a series of tuning slides of varying length and to fix the mouthpipe in position, using the different length tuning slides as crooks. Instruments built in this way were called *cors solo* in

French (plate 74). The fixed mouthpipe avoided all risk of wobble, a considerable advantage for the soloist and it also meant that the bell of the horn was always the same distance from the mouthpiece, again an important consideration for the soloist who needed to be able to control the precise position of his right hand in the bell. Such soloists' horns were limited in the keys in which they could play because it was not practicable to build them short enough to manage the high crooks and any attempt to do so would result in the use of an unacceptable amount of cylindrical tubing for the low crooks, but since the only keys in which solo works were written were from G down to D, and most commonly F, E flat and D, such a restriction was no great disadvantage. The cor solo shown in plate 74 dates from the 1820s, just beyond our period, but it was chosen partly because it was made by the greatest of all horn makers, Lucien-Joseph Raoux, who was working in Paris within our period, and partly because it belonged to the greatest of all horn scholars, the late Reginald Morley Pegge, who first revealed to me, on this instrument, that it was possible to play all the notes of the scale perfectly in tune and absolutely evenly in tone quality and volume from the written middle C to the top of the range with the equipment available to Mozart's and Beethoven's players.

Although soloists would usually play only in these three or four keys, the orchestral players needed to be able to play in all keys, for the harmonic series is useful only when sounded in a key compatible with the key of the music, something that is controlled by the length of the instrument; a horn built in C will be of very little use in a piece of music in D major. Therefore players had always to be equipped with a full set of crooks, and it was precisely on this point that the older system of a couple of master crooks with a set of couplers as shown in plate 75 caused discomfort. Since the position of the mouthpiece is fixed by the player's head, if he were using such a horn he would find that his hand in the bell kept varying its position according to the number of couplers used. With just a master crook, his elbow would be sharply bent and his hand high up against his side; with a master crook and several couplers, his arm might be almost straight and his hand below his thigh. Thus the system of a separate crook for each key became much the more popular. The use of two master crooks and couplers persisted in Britain into the early nineteenth century, but on the Continent the full set of crooks, combined with a tuning slide, became the normal form of the orchestral horn, as in plate 73.

One result of playing with the hand in the bell was that it became necessary to widen the bell-throat; the throat of the older model of horn was too narrow for the hand to produce the best results. This widening of the bell-throat helped to produce a mellower tone quality and throats were widened rather more in Germany, Austro-Bohemia and England than they were in France, a difference that persists to the present day.

The soloist's hand-horn technique required much practice if the tone and the volume were to be even and all notes in tune, which is one reason why we so often hear hand horn playing today with distressing variations in tone and volume, and in some circumstances the resulting quietness of the sound was a disadvantage. Moreover, the hand technique was no substitute for the use of different crooks for performance in different keys. The search for a truly chromatic horn began in around 1760 with Ferdinand Kölbel's invention of the *Amor-Schall*, a horn equipped with woodwind-like keys on or near the bell, an instrument of which no example is known

Plate 74 Cor solo by Lucien-Joseph Raoux, Paris, 1823, with tuning slide crooks for G, F, E, E flat (in the instrument) and D. (*Bate Collection, 67, Oxford University*)

Plate XIII 'Gilles and his family', Antoine Watteau. The guitar as it was played at the French court. (*Wallace Collection, London, 381*)

Plate XIV   Clavichord by Johann Adolf Hass, Hamburg, 1763. FF-f³, double-strung throughout, with extra 4′ strings FF-B. Full-size fret-free clavichord. (*Russell Collection no. 22, Edinburgh University*)

Plate XV   Single-manual harpsichord by John Broadwood, London, 1793, no. 1155. The last-known Broadwood harpsichord. FF-f³, 2 × 8′, 1 × 4′, lute, harp, machine and Venetian swell. One 8′ rank with leather plectra, the other with quill. Left pedal operates the machine stop, right pedal operates the swell. (*Russell Collection no. 19, Edinburgh University*)

to survive. His own performance on this instrument in St Petersburg, where he was a member of the orchestra, is reported to have been successful, but the instrument must have been expensive, and it and its technique were sufficiently complex that it did not attract other makers or players. Hand-stopping remained the normal method for obtaining non-harmonic notes in the middle of the range through the rest of the eighteenth and well into the nineteenth century.

The Trumpet

As with the horn, a change of use was much the most important development of this period; unlike the horn, however, this was not the result of any momentous discovery but of the end of the clarino technique. It is not clear why this happened, whether as older players died off no younger generation of clarinists appeared to succeed them, or whether composers simply stopped writing in this style. Concertos such as that by Leopold Mozart, Wolfgang's father, indicate that the style continued later than is sometimes thought, and if Leopold Mozart wrote in this style there must have been at least one player left to play in it. Several works in the horn repertoire are evidence that the technique and style did not die out completely but survived to a limited extent on that instrument. Nevertheless, it can be said as a generality that with the deaths of Bach and Handel, the clarino trumpet technique almost vanished and was maintained by only a few players. It did survive to a limited extent in England, where Handel's music continued to be performed and where some players continued to use a form of natural trumpet into living memory. The technique is being revived today by those trumpeters who realise that the music of composers who wrote for a certain sonority may benefit from being played with the original instruments and techniques, since only they can produce that sonority; however, as has already been said, there is still an excessive tendency to rely on unauthentic aids such as finger holes. From the middle of the eighteenth century onwards, it was a rare trumpet part that ascended higher than the twelfth harmonic, the G at the top of the treble stave, so that trumpet parts once more became chordal, quasi-fanfare parts with adjacent notes only practicable in the upper fifth of the range.

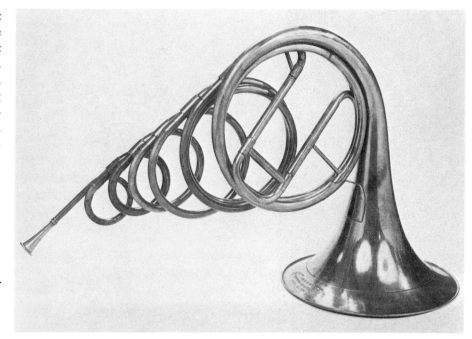

While this was adequate for much of the orchestral music of the period, it was clearly inadequate for any solo work. One attempt to fill out the range of the instrument was by bending the trumpet into a curve so that the player could reach the bell with his hand. These *demi-lune* or *Stopftrompete* (plate 76) are fairly common in collections. It has been suggested that the shape was adopted solely so that the sound would be projected backwards to troops on the march, but enough instruments have survived with wear marks inside the bell to indicate that they were indeed stopped trumpets and that they were played with the same hand-stopping technique as the horn; in addition, some written evidence has survived of this technique. Experiment has suggested that hand-stopping on the trumpet is most effective when the palm of the hand is placed flat across the bell, rather than into it as on the horn, since the smaller bell tends to produce too muffled a tone, but as yet insufficient has been discovered about this technique on the trumpet to reach any firm conclusions. Certainly the wear marks found on some instruments are inside the bells, and we must conclude that at least some players stopped the instrument in this way. Either method of stopping removes the ringing tone that is characteristic of the trumpet, and this would mean either that there was a great tonal difference between stopped

Plate 75 Inventions Horn by William Shaw, London, late 18th century, with master crook and couplers. (*Private Collection*)

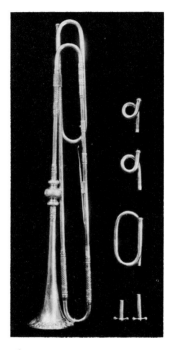

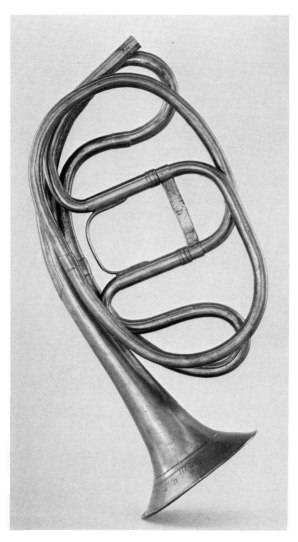

instruments obtaining a full chromatic range. How the player was to sound those notes which such a combination of two harmonic series a semitone apart would still be unable to produce is unexplained; his pamphlet *Musical Phenomena* is quoted in extenso by Morley Pegge in his book *The French Horn* and readers are welcome to see whether they can make any more sense of it than Mr Pegge and the present author have been able to do.

The most successful solution depended upon the use of holes in the tubing, possibly deriving from Kölbel's Amor-Schall and possibly invented independently. Experiment of this sort was much in the air at this time. One example of such experimentation was discovered by Eric Halfpenny in the vaults of St James's Palace in London and is illustrated here (plate 77) by gracious permission of Her Majesty The Queen. This is a trumpet by William Shaw dated 1787 and provided with three finger holes which can be covered with rotating sleeves, and a fourth hole which is covered by a key. However, this instrument is quite different from a key trumpet, for the holes are in different positions and have a much smaller diameter. Experimenting with the instrument, Eric Halfpenny found that these holes were harmonic vents of the sort found on one or two surviving baroque trumpets which, when uncovered, raise the pitch of the instrument by a fifth and allow it to produce a second harmonic series. The Shaw trumpet is unique in having four vents instead of the usual single one; that it has so many is explained by the set of crooks with which it is provided, for each vent works with a different crook. Thus the vent nearest to the player and to the bell allows the player to play, without a crook, in E flat or in the B flat above; the second vent gives A with the D crooks, of which there are two, one slightly flatter than the other; the third allows the C crook to produce the G series, and the keyed vent gives F on the B flat crook. Thus a trumpet with only three crooks can play in eight keys, but it could not produce any more notes in those keys than could any other natural trumpet.

Apart from this instrument, and a number of vague and maddeningly frustrating references (most of which will be found in Reine Dahlqvist's study) nothing at all definite is known before 1796, the year in which Haydn wrote his Trumpet Concerto,

and open notes or that the normal trumpet tone quality was absent throughout the performance. The lack of any quantity of music requiring this technique suggests that hand-stopping was not really successful or much liked, a suggestion that is confirmed by the continuous attempts to find some other method of obtaining the non-harmonic notes; the paucity of information and the lack of any surviving instruments is an indication that most of these attempts ended in failure.

One frustratingly vague description is that in Clagget's patent of 1788 for a miscellany of instruments, among which he suggests uniting two horns or two trumpets, one a semitone higher than the other, and by judicious alternation between the two

which is indubitably for a key trumpet (plate 78). The writing, particularly the witty contrasts between the two natural trumpets in the orchestra and the chromatic soloist who is quite clearly saying 'Listen to what I can do and you can't do', suggests that the instrument was new and perhaps was being shown off for the first time. However, it is obvious that a work of such considerable virtuosity cannot be played unless the performer is fully at home with his instrument, and of course he must have been able to show Haydn what was possible and most effective on the instrument before the work could be written. Thus it seems fair to say that there was an efficient and effective key trumpet in existence early in the 1790s and that Weidinger, who is known to have been the soloist though he is not now thought to have been the inventor of the instrument, was a player of considerable ability.

There is some evidence, especially in Italian opera scores, that the key trumpet became quite widely used, but this was not until the early years of the nineteenth century, the period from which most of the surviving instruments, including that shown in plate 78, derive, a period beyond our present scope. The normal orchestral instrument of the latter half of the eighteenth century was the natural trumpet in E flat, equipped, as has been described above, with crooks to take it down to B flat. This shortening of the instrument from the C trumpet used at the beginning of the seventeenth century to a D trumpet at the end of it and now to E flat, with F becoming the normal basic pitch early in the nineteenth century, is something that has continued into our own time. It happens partly because it is somewhat easier to get high notes on a shorter instrument; the note sounding the B flat nearly two octaves above middle C will be easier as a twelfth harmonic on the E flat trumpet than as a sixteenth harmonic on a B flat trumpet, but this reason becomes more important in the next century with the invention of valves. In the eighteenth century, the main inducement was simply the need to avoid carrying several trumpets around. It is possible to have both a C trumpet and a D trumpet; or to have a D trumpet with a whole tone crook to convert it into a C trumpet. It is not possible, however, to have a C trumpet from which enough tubing can be removed to convert it into a D trumpet. Therefore, if a player wishes to use trumpets in keys

higher than C or D, he must have a shorter instrument but one that can be lengthened with crooks to bring it back to those keys. At the end of the eighteenth century, E flat was the highest key in which trumpets were used.

This wish to play in more keys and to use the trumpet more widely in orchestras was furthered by the gradual break-up of the trumpet guilds. The rules and restrictions that had forbidden anyone who was not a member of the guild and who had not served the appropriate apprenticeship to play the trumpet, and that had strictly controlled who was allowed to employ trumpeters, whether on a permanent or a temporary basis, were becoming less and less observed. It is a matter for conjecture whether the guilds were no longer thought necessary because, with the end of the clarino technique, there were no longer any secrets that could only be learned through apprenticeship in the guild, or whether the clarino technique died out because there were no longer any apprentices learning it in the guilds. It may well be that both cause and effect operated simultaneously, for the changing social structure was already breaking up the strict apprenticeship method of learning a trade in all walks of life and not just in trumpet playing, and all the medieval guilds were disappearing.

The important results for musical history were that trumpeters were much more freely available for normal orchestral work and that composers were no longer restricted to writing for trumpets only on the occasions when they would have been permitted to play under the guild system. Because trumpets were more often employed, they had to be able to play in more keys, and thus the new and shorter instruments came into use. Presumably the

Plate 78 Key trumpet in A flat, anonymous, probably South German or Austrian, c. 1830, with five keys, all for the left hand. (*Rück Collection, Germanisches Nationalmuseum, Nürnberg, MIR 129*)

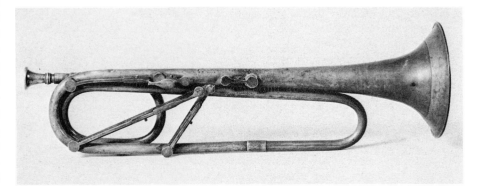

E flat trumpet was the highest on which it was comfortable for normal players to produce the twelfth harmonic, and the B flat the lowest on which it was easy to produce a proper trumpet tone (the instrument was the same tube length as a tenor trombone). When composers wrote in keys outside this range, in F, G or A, they either reconciled themselves to doing without trumpets, or they wrote for them in the nearest available crooking and wrote only such notes as were compatible with the keys of the music and the instrument. Doing without them was less serious than it had been, for whereas in the first half of the eighteenth and much of the seventeenth centuries the trumpet had been the only brass instrument available for melodic use in the orchestra, the horn, with its sound now moderated to something which would blend with other instruments and with the possibility of the occasional hand-stopped note to fill an awkward gap, was the more important of the two. Trumpeters, while never descending quite to the low esteem with which orchestral horn players had been regarded in the previous period, had to take a back seat until the invention of the valves once again put them back into their proper place as the upper voice of the brass choir.

The Trombone

The trombone, partly because it was still so little used outside the church, changed only slightly in the middle of the century. It was perhaps at this time that the bell of the instrument became slightly more flared, though it is difficult to be sure, for although the sackbut is regarded as an instrument with an almost conical bell (compared with the later trombone with almost a modern flared bell), there are sackbuts with flared bells. Equally, there are sackbuts with stockings at the ends of the slides, though this is rare. Obviously the inner legs of a trombone slide must fit fairly closely within the tubing of the slide in order to avoid air leakage, but there are mechanical disadvantages in moving two close-fitting telescopic tubes against each other. Mechanically it is much easier if only the final extremity of the legs is a close fit, with the rest of the tubing having a greater clearance. This close fit was provided by soldering an extra layer of metal called a stocking round the end of each leg. In this period the flat, removable stays joining one branch of the slide tubing to its neighbour finally gave way to fixed tubular stays. Again, it is difficult to say precisely when this happened, for a number of earlier instruments also have a flat stay in the bell bow and tubular stays on the slide, and we cannot tell whether these tubular stays were original or whether they are the result of later repair. Certainly the flat stay adds a useful stiffness to the bell joint, which is probably why it was retained, and because the slide stays are gripped by the hand, players may have changed to these because they found a round stay more comfortable than a flat one.

Trombones came back into common secular use in the military bands and in the opera orchestra in the last quarter of the eighteenth century. They had been used in the operas of Monteverdi and his contemporaries, at least on the special occasions for which a large orchestra was engaged, but, as we have seen, the majority of seventeenth century operas and masques were written for small bands consisting of various types of strings and keyboards. In the latter part of the eighteenth century, the opera orchestra expanded in size just as the concert orchestra had done, and the trombones quickly became members of these operatic orchestras even though they were seldom used in ordinary concerts. Thus Mozart seems to have used trombones only in his operatic scores and occasionally in religious works. The trombones had never ceased to be members of church choirs and this religious connexion continued outside the church as well as in it, so that the orchestra for a large ceremonial setting of the Mass would often include trombones and so would the orchestra for oratorios such as Haydn's *The Creation*.

Because their main task was to accompany voices, the normal group of trombones was a set of three: alto, tenor and bass (plate 79). The uppermost part, which would have been played by a cornett in the sixteenth and seventeenth centuries, seems usually to have been left unsupported. This would have caused little difficulty in the latter part of the eighteenth century, partly because, when an orchestra was used, other instruments would almost certainly be playing the upper line, and partly because the uppermost part now normally carried the tune and was thus more easily learned and more easily sung without support than the lower parts, which were mainly harmonic in character rather than melodic. Certainly the soprano trombone existed, but as at all other periods it was little used. Perhaps this was a matter of tone quality, for the soprano trombone has little of the majestic grandeur of sound of the larger instruments, nor would it add to the solemnity of ecclesiastical ceremonies.

The other main use of the trombones was in the military bands. These were a new phenomenon in the eighteenth century, for previously a flute and drum or a group of such instruments had usually sufficed for keeping time and encouraging troops on the march, and military signals, before the days of field telephones and walkie-talkies, had been passed by trumpet, bugle or drum. Now regiments began to vie with one another in providing military music. This was still an unofficial matter, however, and military bands were not part of the official establishment of a regiment but were normally in the private employ of the Colonel of the Regiment or of the officers as a group, who would pay their wages and provide their uniforms and, presumably, their instruments. As a result, the combinations of instruments in such bands varied widely according to the financial means and the musical tastes of the officers' mess. Quite a common basic combination was the pairs of oboes, clarinets, bassoons and horns which has already been referred to in connexion with serenades and such music, and varying numbers and varieties of instruments, frequently among them a group of trombones, were added to this.

The Serpent

Another common member of these new military bands was the serpent. This had the advantage of having a brass-type mouthpiece, of possessing a sonorous and carrying voice, and of being provided with finger holes which enabled it to play a fully diatonic part in the bass. Thus it could strengthen and support the bass line of the band and reinforce the bassoons, which were rather too weak to play without such support out of doors. Being made of quite thin wood, the serpent is lighter than it looks and it was not too heavy or difficult to carry on the march. A number of parts survive in military music labelled contrafagotto and it is far more likely that these were played on the serpent than on the double bassoon; it is normally assumed that where no separate part

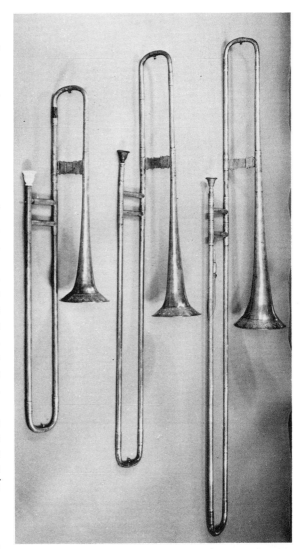

Plate 79 TROMBONES. *Left to right:* alto in E flat, tenor in B flat, bass in F, anonymous, German, 1814. One of the few surviving sets of trombones. (*Bate Collection, 730, 731, 732. Oxford University*)

existed the serpent doubled the second bassoon part.

The serpent was also still commonly used in churches to support the bass voices and the normal name for the continental keyless serpent (such as that on the left of plate 80) is *serpent d'église* or church serpent. This was still usually built with somewhat open curves, in a shape much like that of the earlier periods. In Britain, however, the curves were taken round a much smaller radius, producing an instrument which was more compact and more easily carried on the march (plate 80, centre). It is said to have been George III who suggested that the bell should be turned outwards, partly the better to project the sound and partly to make it slightly easier

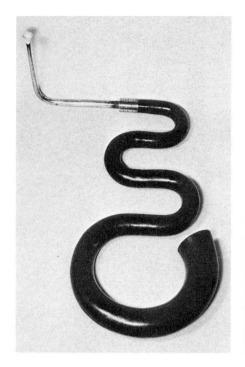

Plate 80 SERPENTS. *Left to right:* serpent d'église, no keys, anonymous, French, 18th century; serpent, 3 keys, anonymous, English, *c.* 1800; bass horn, anonymous but probably by Louis Alexandre Frichot in London in the 1790s, 3 keys. (*Carse Collection, Horniman Museum, London, 14.5.47/223, /317, /284*)

to carry; certainly it is from the latter part of the eighteenth century that English serpents were made with the bell turned slightly outwards. Like the woodwind instruments, the serpent was provided with keys, usually three or four, to help it to produce chromatic notes. However, as Morley Pegge points out in his article on the instrument, these keys were of little help unless the player already had a good ear; the serpent is naturally so flexible in pitch that, unless the player was able to play the note in tune to start with, the only effect of a key is to provide another out-of-tune fingering. This flexibility has bedevilled several makers of reproduction instruments; many of the cheaper examples, especially some of those made of modern materials, such as fibreglass, are so flexible in intonation that it is impossible for even a good player to centre any of the notes at all.

By the end of the century, makers were beginning to experiment with other and more portable shapes of the instrument. Frichot produced the original model of his bass horn, an example of which can be seen on the right of plate 80, in about 1790 while he was living in London as a refugee from the French Revolution, and slightly earlier Régibo was experimenting with his upright model, which led to the Russian bassoon (neither Russian nor a bassoon, but

a serpent built in a shape not unlike that of the bassoon), an instrument which, like the later pattern of the bass horn, is more characteristic of the nineteenth century than of the eighteenth and must be left to future consideration.

Percussion Instruments

One of the purposes of a military band is that it should catch and impress the eye as well as the ear, and regiments vied with each other in the selection of their uniforms and the use of novelties and exotica. The favourite exotic flavour was provided by imitation Turkish music, often played by negroes though never, so far as is known, by real Turks. Perhaps this was appropriate, for the Janissary bands of the Turkish army, on which this music was based, were also, in theory at least, not manned by Turks but by captured Christians and their descendants. The European military band was often led by a jingling johnnie (plate 81), an instrument made in several shapes but always consisting of a pole surmounted by bells. A frequent pattern consists of two metal arms from which a number of pellet bells, or sometimes small real bells, were suspended; above this was a metal cone in the shape of a Chinese coolie's hat (hence the French name for the instrument of *chapeau chinois*), from the rim of which further bells were suspended, and above all a metal crescent, whence the alternative English name of Turkish crescent. All these metal parts were mounted on metal sleeves sufficiently loosely fitted on the wooden pole that as it was lifted and thumped on the ground at every step, the whole instrument shook and rattled. Its use presents a musical problem, for it is never mentioned in the scores, though Berlioz does score for it in the middle of the following century, and one often wonders whether it should be used in such works as Haydn's *Military Symphony* and if so, what it should play. Another instrument often seen in illustrations of military bands but which also never appears in scores is the tambourine, apparently not much changed from its medieval form, save that the jingles are somewhat smaller and lighter, though still larger and heavier than those of the modern instrument. Yet another is the side drum, which again is seldom written into the music even though it almost invariably appears in the pictures.

The side drum (plate 82) was by now considerably smaller than that used in the late sixteenth century, described by Arbeau as being two-and-a-half feet in diameter and the same in depth, and that of the early seventeenth century, such as the drum in the Tower of London, described in detail in my books on early percussion, and which is only half a foot smaller. It was, however, still considerably larger than the modern instrument. Continental instruments had a tension screw for the snares, as can already be seen on Praetorius's illustration (our plate 20), which shows a side drum of much the same size as that in the Tower. English drums, however, usually simply had the snare fixed between the flesh hoop on which the skin is lapped and the counter hoop through which the tension cords are passed, either just with a knot in each end so that it would not come out, or sewn and knotted through a strip of leather to hold it. The snares seem, if those on surviving examples are any indication, to be considerably lighter and thinner than those which can be seen knotted on the drum in Rembrandt's *The Night Watch*, though still very much heavier than those in use today, and the absence of a tension screw suggests that the sound was probably a much looser rattle than the modern snap, though it must nevertheless have been sufficiently definite to keep the footmen in step. The

Plate 81 Jingling johnnie (chapeau chinois), anonymous, France, late 18th century, with pellet bells and true bells. (*Fryklund Collection, Musikmuseet, Stockholm*)

Plate 82 Side drum,
anonymous, England, early
18th century. Photographed
upside down to show the
snares. (*Snowshill Manor,
National Trust, Gal.119*)

Plate 83 Tenor drum,
anonymous, probably English,
late 18th century. Ferrous
metal shell. Unrestored.
(*Author's Collection, II 192*)

snare, of course, ran below the lower head of the drum; the instrument in plate 82 has been photographed upside down so that the snare can be seen.

Another drum appearing in pictures of the period is the tenor drum. Today that instrument is a large side drum without snares, but in the eighteenth century it was a single small timpano, a small kettledrum carried at the player's waist, often played, if the pictures can be trusted, by a black boy. Surviving examples are very rare, the only one known to the author being that shown in plate 83, which is, as yet, unrestored.

The instruments used in the orchestra were the bass drum, triangle and cymbals. It was enough to include these in a score and immediately the hearers either thought of the panoplies of war or were transported to exotic places, as they were by Mozart in the overture of his opera *Die Entführung aus dem Serail*, by Michael Haydn, Joseph's brother, in his *Turkish Suite*, or by many young ladies when by pressing a pedal they brought into play the Turkish instruments built into their pianos.

The bass drum was an imitation of the Turkish *davul*, a large drum rather deeper from head to head than its diameter, played with two different beaters, a heavy club and a light stick. In Europe the long drum (plate 84), as it was called, was deeper than the davul and there was no snare. The drum was suspended horizontally across the player's chest, the player being the tallest man who could be found. The drum was beaten on one head with a solid club like that of the davul and on the other, instead of the thin stick of the Turkish original, with a switch of birch twigs, like that used for chastising children and indeed, perhaps, the same switch as that used for disciplining the drummer boys. Composers specified the use of the two beaters and this was clearly indicated in the music by the direction of the stems of the notes on the bass drum part and can still be seen in reputable editions of such works as the *Military Symphony* and those mentioned in the previous paragraph. This distinction in intended sound is quite lost today when the music is played on a modern bass drum with the normal felt-headed or lambswool beater.

The sound of the other instruments is also distorted today, for the eighteenth century cymbals, while larger than those of the Renaissance, were con-

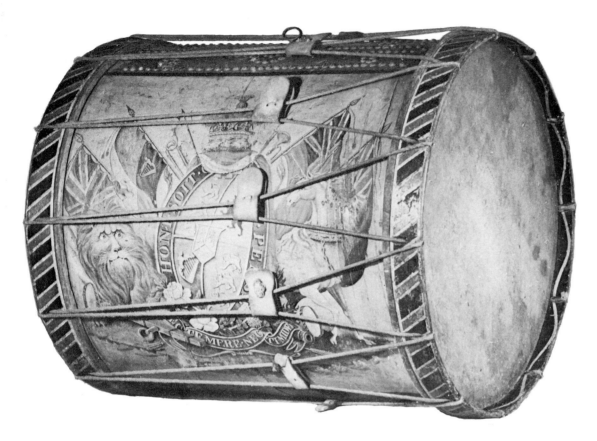

Plate 84 Long drum (bass drum), anonymous, probably English, 18th century. (*Snowshill Manor, National Trust, Gal.118*)

siderably smaller and thicker than those used today, and the triangle still had the rings which had been normal in medieval times. The rapid reiteration of cymbal strokes, which was common in this music, was effective and rhythmic with contemporary cymbals but sets up an intolerable mushy clangour with the modern instruments. The contemporary triangle, on the other hand, produced a continuous susurration, as the rings jingled against the frame, quite different from the rhythmic tinkle of the modern instrument, which in this context is more reminiscent of a telephone than a military band. In addition to these tonal differences, the modern instruments are much louder than those of the eighteenth century so that the whole internal balance of the orchestra is upset.

A few other percussion instruments appeared in the dance music, divertimenti and other lighter works of various composers. Sleigh rides, a popular feature of such music, were accompanied by sets of tuned sleigh bells, just as post horns were brought in for special effects now and again. It seems to have been true at all periods that percussion instruments make their way into the orchestra from military bands and from dance bands, but it is only towards the end of the two centuries covered by this book that we see returning to formal music any of the percussion instruments that had been so popular in the Middle Ages and early Renaissance. That they and others had existed as folk instruments throughout this period is apparent from books such as Bonanni's *Gabinetto Armonico*, from which plates 85 and 86 are taken, which shows many of the percussion instruments we have already encountered in the previous book still in common use among peasants and folk musicians in many areas. Plate 85 shows the tambourine played, as it usually is in folk music, by a woman. Plate 86 shows one child with a pair of

LXXIII *Timpano Moderno*

XCVI *Instrumenti Fanciulleschi*

Plate 85 Tambourine played by a woman dancer, early 18th century. (*Filippo Bonanni, Gabinetto Armonico, Rome, 1722*)

Plate 86 Children playing bones (seated; another pair rests on the boulder beside the boy) and stones (standing). (*Bonanni*)

stones, common percussion instruments in many parts of the world, and the other with a pair of bones, an instrument which can still be heard as a folk instrument today. Bonanni was exceptional among writers of books on musical instruments of any age for his interest in folk instruments and the instruments of non-European musical cultures, and his book is an essential tool for any study of these subjects, but it does have to be treated with some care and cross-checked with actual instruments and other sources.

The Timpani

The only percussion instruments to be used as ordinary orchestral instruments without exotic or military connotations were still the timpani (plate 87), and it is difficult to be sure how much they changed at this time. Few instruments are dated and although a considerable number survive in collections, they are mainly in collections of arms and other such appurtenances of noble splendour and status. While the scores of all the composers of the period make it clear that the timpani were widely used for musical

performances of all sorts, we can never be sure whether any existing pairs of drums were used for orchestral or ceremonial purposes. It is indeed likely that the same pair was often used for both and that when the court orchestra, or any other orchestra, played a work using timpani, the serjeant-drummer was called in, bringing the drums from the armoury with him, for even though the public concerts were now a normal feature of civilised life in all the great cities of Europe, the princely and episcopal courts were still the main employers of musicians and composers. Many of the musicians who played in the public concerts were able to do so only by permission of their full-time employer, for they still depended upon the security of a position in a nobleman's private orchestra as the mainstay of their livelihood. In such orchestras, the timpani would almost inevitably be those which were also used for ceremonial occasions.

The drums appear to have increased in size during this period, from around fifty or fifty-five centimetres in diameter to something nearer the later sixty-two and seventy centimetres, and perhaps because of this increase we hear less of the double drums; once the single drums had grown to this size there was less need for anything larger. Sticks remained hard, normally discs of wood but occasionally of hard leather and only occasionally covered with soft leather. It is not until the second quarter of the nineteenth century that Berlioz writes of the new sticks with soft heads, and all timpani parts of the eighteenth century and through Beethoven's lifetime in the nineteenth century were played with hard-headed sticks, which make a very different sound from those we hear today.

The break-up of the trumpeters' guilds also affected timpanists, for both were members of the same guilds and normally played together. Although the timpani occasionally appeared without the trumpets, as in Mozart's *Serenata Notturna* for strings and timpani, on the whole old habits died hard and the timpani were normally written for as though they were bass trumpets, just as they had been throughout the period covered by this book. Haydn, who is said to have been a timpanist, was the first among the great composers to write really independent and effective parts and his are by far the best and the most rewarding to play of all those written in his lifetime. But it was Beethoven who early in the nineteenth century broke away from the standard tonic and dominant tunings and who was the first to write really difficult parts for the timpanist, the most exacting of which are those in his first and last symphonies; the so-called minuet of the first symphony, which goes as fast as any of the later scherzos, is and must always have been a timpanist's nightmare.

String Instruments

The Violin

The members of the violin family changed less than any other instruments in the middle of the century, but there was a difference in the way in which the instrument was held. Whereas it had been held against the breast and, later, on the shoulder or collar-bone as Geminiani suggested in his tutor in 1751, Leopold Mozart in 1756 recommended either the latter position or, and much more strongly as by far the better position, gripped by the chin, much as we hold it today save that the chin came on the other side of the tail-piece. Later in the century other preceptors recommend gripping it on the same side of the tail-piece as the modern grip, though of course without the chin rest, which had not yet been invented. The violin itself remained much the same as it had been.

During the latter part of the century, however, the greater number of wind instruments available led quite quickly to the need for louder and larger string bands to balance them. A permanent princely musical establishment characteristic of most music making in the middle of the century was often quite small: there would be a nucleus of string instruments, a couple of horn players (who were also huntsmen), a couple of trumpeters and a drummer (who were officially part of the ceremonial establishment of the princely house but available to the musical side of the household on request), a bassoon or two, and a pair of oboists who could, especially if the music were not too complicated, double on flutes There are a great many works written in the 1750s and 1760s in which the oboes of the quick opening and closing movements give way to flutes in the slow movement. However, when an orchestra was employed for a public concert and paid for by the tickets of some hundreds of people, it was possible and desirable to employ a larger number. Such orchestras included both flutes and oboes, as well as a pair of the new clarinets, plus a pair each of bassoons, horns and trumpets, and a drummer. To balance such a wind section, much greater power was needed from the string band, at first from the violin itself, followed by the viola, cello and double bass. There was no need for any change to ensure greater expression— the violin was already capable of any nuance within the imagination of the player, as a glance at Geminiani's treatise on playing the instrument reveals. It is this instruction book which casts the greatest doubt upon the claim that the crescendo and diminuendo, the idea of a line of music swelling and dwindling in loudness, were invented at Mannheim, for Geminiani, writing in 1751 but representing the violin school of Corelli whose pupil he had been, castigates any playing without such alterations of loudness as bad and unmusical. Sheer power of volume was another matter, however. The baroque bow, with its long slender point, could draw a magical translucency of tone and clarity of line from the strings, but it could not produce a strong attack, the *coup d'archet* or stroke of the bow, desired by Mozart and his contemporaries; as many composers observed, the only way to stop an audience from gossiping and make them listen to the music was to begin by startling them with a good thumping chord, and this chord was called the *coup d'archet*. Nor was the violin itself well constructed for the *coup d'archet*, for the gut strings on the low, only slightly arched bridge could not be attacked with any great force lest, since their tension was far lower than it is today, they sank so far under the bow-stroke that the bow hairs touched the neighbouring string and introduced unwanted notes into the harmony.

Bows were therefore modified, the head becoming heavier and holding the hairs further from the wood, allowing the player to apply full power right out to the tip where in the past the hair had been too near the wood for this to be possible. The stick itself, which had been straight or even outwardly curved, was bent slightly towards the hair in the centre, thus producing a far stronger construction and allowing the bow hair to be tightened far more, thus again increasing the strength with which the player could attack the string. In part, this new construction of the bow was aided by a commercial accident. Among the imports of the new commercial empires was indigo from Brazil, which was shipped in barrels made of a cheap and convenient local wood called pernambuco from its place of origin, and it was discovered that this wood, which would otherwise have been burned or thrown away, was ideal for violin bows, and all good bows are made from it to this day, though no longer, alas, from broken-up barrels but from specially, and expensively, imported

Plate 88   VIOLINS. *Above:*
attributed to Hans Krouchdaler,
Oberbalm, second half 17th
century, in original state;
bridge and tuning pegs are
reconstructions (see plate 4,
left, for front view). *Below:* by
Pietro Antonio Bellone, Milan,
1692, completely modernised
(see text for details).
(*Musikinstrumente Museum,
Berlin, 4519 & 5050*)

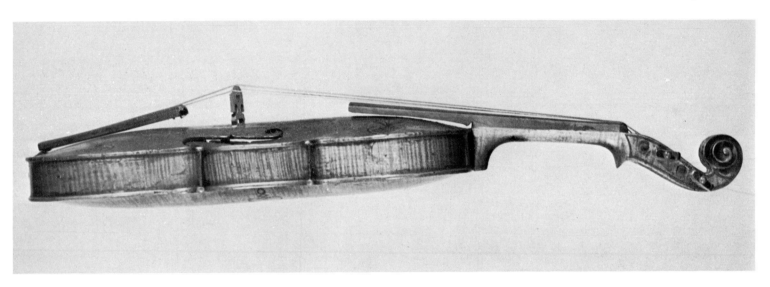

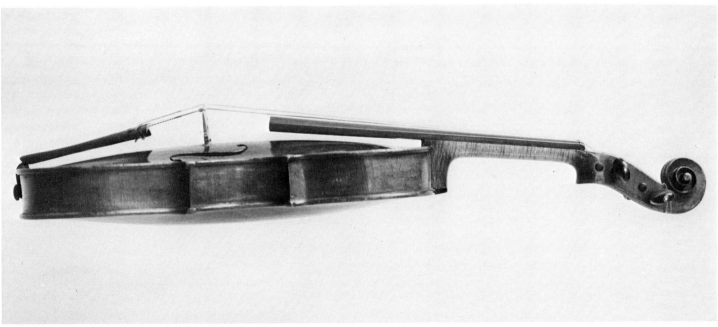

timber. Many makers contributed to the modifications of the bow, the greatest and most important of whom were John Dodd in England and, above all, the younger François Tourte of Paris, who is today regarded as the Stradivarius of bow-makers and whose bows are still supreme and much sought-after. François Tourte's final pattern did not emerge until about 1780, but throughout this period the gradual change was taking place and slowly the older patterns were vanishing from the orchestra, being replaced by the newer and more powerful models.

The changes in the instrument itself were even more radical. It has always been held that a greater tension of the string will produce a greater volume and a brighter sound, and this increase in tension was sought in several ways. One obvious way was simply to wind the tuning pegs tighter, which equally obviously led to a rise in pitch. This rise was fiercely resisted by wind players, who could not wind up their instruments, nor even just cut little bits off without throwing the rest of the instrument out of tune, and also by singers who suffered considerable strain and discomfort at the top of their range. The string players would not be gainsaid, however, and during the second half of the eighteenth century the pitch of most orchestras rose by a semitone or more, so that by 1800 the pitch in London was the same as it is today and in other places it was higher still.

However, objections to this higher pitch came also from string instrument makers and repairers, for the high tension was pulling instruments to pieces. A violin built to withstand a certain strain from the string tension will not, over any great length of time, tolerate much increase in this strain and will try to fold itself up. The great violin makers had attached the neck to the body of the violin simply by driving nails through a block concealed in the top of the body into the root of the neck, and on many instruments the neck was ripped from these nails by the increased pull of the strings. Various modifications were introduced, chief among them that the neck was mortised into the block, so producing a far stronger joint, and that the neck was canted backwards to allow it to bear a far greater strain before it began to give, just as in a tug-of-war the men on the rope will lean backwards to give themselves a better mechanical angle with which to counter the pull. In the past, a violin would rest on a table with its back fully touching it and the scroll at the end of the neck just resting on it; now the new angle of the neck pushed the scroll back so that the scroll lifts the back from the table save for the bottom-most edge. The upper instrument in plate 88 still retains its original neck; the lower has undergone this conversion.

This alteration of the angle of the neck had further results. Because the bridge holds the strings up from the belly of the violin, the fingerboard must also rise from the nut, following the angle of the strings; otherwise, as the player used higher positions he would need to press the strings further and further down towards the fingerboard, thus making playing much more difficult and distorting the tone and the pitch. On the old violin the rise of the fingerboard was achieved by the use of a wedge between the upper surface of the neck and the underside of the fingerboard (plate 88, upper), so that the thumb on the back of the neck and the finger on the string drew further and further apart as the player moved into the higher positions. As Yehudi Menuhin commented, on the first occasion that he played an eighteenth century violin in its original state when he opened the Galpin Society's 21st Anniversary Exhibition in Edinburgh in 1968, this has a double effect. It helps the player to establish the correct position along the string, since as one knows from comparing the thickness of two pieces of paper between finger and thumb, the hand is very sensitive to subtle differences of spacing. Also, as the hand moves back down the fingerboard towards the scroll, it squeezes the violin into the neck or the shoulder, thus making the use of a chin-rest unnecessary, which counters one of the theoretical objections to the lack of a chin-rest—that it made shifting downwards difficult.

Because the neck was now canted backwards, there was no longer any need for this wedge between the neck and the fingerboard, and the back of the neck and the fingerboard were made parallel (plate 88, lower). This did indeed make difficulties in shifting downwards from one position to another and it was this that necessitated Spohr's invention of the chin-rest in the 1820s to help the player to grip the violin between chin and shoulder and hold it steady while the hand moved back and forth on the neck. Because

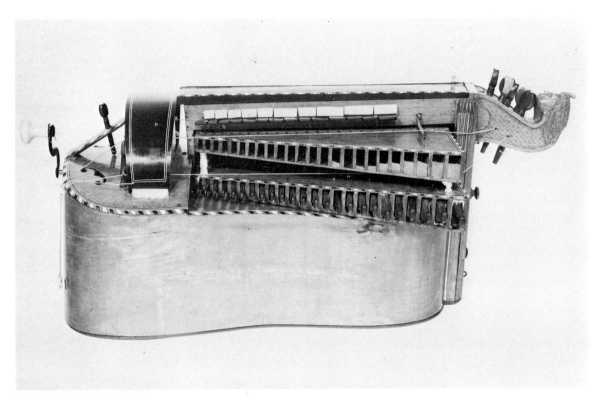

this new thinner fingerboard and neck allowed greater freedom to the hand, the fingerboard was lengthened, as can be seen on the lower instrument in plate 88, enabling the players to play higher notes and so, particularly in solo passages, to display greater brilliance.

The tension of the strings was also increased by raising the bridge, slightly increasing its arch to ensure greater separation of the strings. The bridge, of course, carries the weight, the downward pressure of the strings, and this weight is imparted by the bridge to the belly of the instrument. It was found that the greatly increased weight caused by the higher string tension was imperilling the belly itself, which was supported both by an increase in the thickness of the soundpost, the column standing under one foot of the bridge that holds the belly and the back apart and that at the same time transmits the vibrations of the belly to the back, and by an increase in the thickness and the length of the bass-bar, the girder that runs along inside the belly of the instrument under the other foot of the bridge.

In addition to these changes, at the same time that it was re-angled and reset into the top block, the neck was lengthened slightly, resulting in a slightly longer string length. Since the pitch remained the same at the new high levels, this again meant an increase in the string tension because if a longer string is to produce the same pitch as a shorter one of the same material, the longer one must be tighter.

None of these changes was taken as a giant step, nor were all of them carried out on all violins simultaneously. As with the bow, it was a gradual process and the orchestra of about 1800 must have seen a considerable variety of instruments, some old, some new and some at intermediate stages. However, by the end of the eighteenth century there were enough new ones for the tone and the volume of the string band to be quite different from what they had been in the middle of the century, and the sound of an orchestra playing for Beethoven was totally different from the sound of an orchestra playing for Stamitz in Mannheim.

What is more important in many ways, and what is not generally recognised today, is how much the individual instruments had been changed. A Stradivarius violin, once it had been through these changes, bore little resemblance in sound or in appearance to the instrument which had left the workshop in Cremona. The bridge was new, differently shaped and higher. The neck had either been lengthened or had been replaced with a new one and set at a new angle. The fingerboard was new, longer and more rounded from side to side to match the new curve of the bridge. The bass-bar was new, longer than the old one and more than twice as thick. The soundpost was new and again twice as thick. The strings were screwed to a higher tension and were longer, and some were covered with an over-winding of fine wire. All that survived from the hand of the master was the wooden box and, usually, the scroll at the end of the neck. It says a great deal for his consummate skill and craftmanship that, with all these modifications, which include a change in the sound that is desired from the instrument, this wooden box still produces a sound that is supreme even above those that were designed and made to match the modern fittings.

The Viola d'Amore

After a century or so of fairly casual use by amateur players and others, the use of sympathetic strings on bowed instruments became widely popular all over Europe. Perhaps it was that the shimmer of added harmonies appealed to the ears of the seekers after the new expressionism in music. The instruments on which they were used were the viola d'amore and the baryton. The viola d'amore (plate XI) could be described either as a shallow-bodied treble viol or as a fairly large viola, sometimes made in the shape of either of those instruments and sometimes with a festooned or other fanciful shape of body; it usually had flame-shaped sound holes instead of those of the more usual C or long S or F shape. The depth of the body was that of the viola, rather than that of the viol, because the instrument was held at the shoulder like a viola, and the fingerboard carried no frets. The finial of the pegbox was commonly the head of a woman or of a blindfolded boy, the Cupid whose eyes are hid that he may not see where his darts of love will land. There were usually six or seven bowed strings with a varying number, commonly between five and seven, of sympathetic strings of wire running below them through a tunnel under the fingerboard and through a lower opening of the bridge. The viola d'amore seems to have been exclusively a solo and chamber music instrument; it never appeared as a member of the orchestra.

The Baryton

Equally an instrument for solos and chamber music was the baryton, a memorable instrument because its best known player was Haydn's patron and employer Count Esterházy (plate XII). Because it was one of every court composer's duties to provide his patron with music if the patron were himself a player, there remains a corpus of superb music for this instrument. The baryton is a form of bass viol, normally with six bowed strings and normally without frets on the fingerboard. It is usually of festooned shape so that it can be stood upright on its base. There are a considerable number of sympathetic strings, anything from a dozen to forty, and, unlike those of the viola d'amore, these sympathetic strings run not only behind the fingerboard but also beside it. The back of the neck is open so that the player can pluck these strings with the left thumb at the same time as he is bowing and fingering the six main strings. The only instrument with which it can be compared in this respect is the Indian sitar, which also has sympathetic strings that can be plucked as well as left to resonate in sympathy with the sounds of the main strings. The baryton has a beautiful sound and the quality of its surviving music is so high that it is a continual surprise that players have been so slow to revive it today.

The Lira

Another instrument for which Haydn wrote a good deal of music also awaits revival, but one suspects that such revival will be much slower in coming, if indeed anybody bothers to revive it at all. This is the lira organizzata (plate 89), the favourite instrument of the King of Naples, who was also one of Haydn's patrons and with whom, incidentally, Admiral Lord Nelson had dealings, for Lady Hamilton was the wife of the British Ambassador to that monarch's court.

The lira was a hurdy-gurdy, a string instrument bowed by a revolving wheel, combined with a miniature organ. One hesitates to say that an instrument which one has never heard must have sounded extraordinary, but nevertheless an instrument that combines what was in effect a portative organ in perpetual unison with a rather snarling bowed string, accompanied without surcease by a multiple string drone, would seem to merit such description.

The Hurdy-Gurdy

The sight of a hurdy-gurdy in royal hands was not, perhaps, surprising, for during the eighteenth century it had quite lost its reputation, acquired from the Renaissance onwards, of being an instrument suited only to blind beggars. It had been ideal for them, for both the bow, consisting of a wheel turned by a crank, and the fingerboard, consisting of a row of keys, were easily operated by those who could not see what they were doing nor where their hands and fingers were placed, and there are many genre paintings and engravings showing this use. Because it was so firmly associated with beggars and the blind, the hurdy-gurdy had disappeared from serious music, though it had survived as a folk instrument in country districts over much of Europe, and it is known today as a folk instrument from France to Hungary and, in a variant form, in Sweden. Perhaps the French court had become bored with the bag-pipes and the guitar; perhaps any new sensation was seized upon with avidity. Whatever the reason, the hurdy-gurdy or *vielle à roue* (plate 90) became suddenly popular at the court, probably the more easily because the sound of drones was familiar from the musette. Many lutes were destroyed so that their backs might be made into the body of the newly fashionable instrument, for it was sometimes made with a lute body (*vielle en luth*) and sometimes with that of a guitar (*vielle en guitare*).

Plate 90 shows the same instrument twice: the upper view is as it appears in use and the lower shows it with the wheel-guard off so that the wheel can be seen, and with the tangent box open so that the keys and tangents are visible. The commonest arrangement, as on this instrument, was to have six strings, two of which were melody strings or chanterelles passing through the tangent or key box, and four of which were drones, usually passing down the outside of the box but occasionally with one or more inside it. All six strings crossed the wheel and sounded the whole time unless the player drew one or two of the drones away from the wheel so that they would not sound. The trumpet drone was the one which was most often removed in this way, for it passed over a

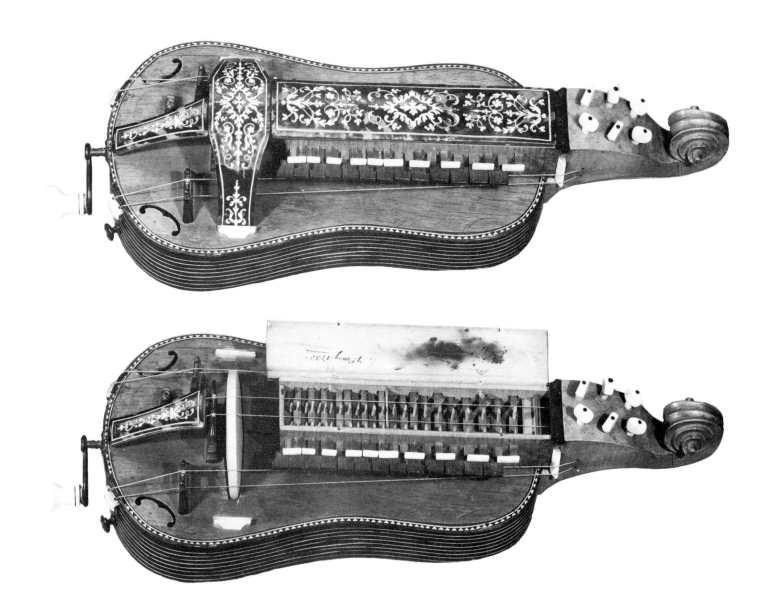

Plate 90 Hurdy-gurdy (vielle à roue) by Georges Louvet, Paris, 1733. Two chanterelles, four drones. The lower picture shows the same instrument with the tangent box open and the wheel guard removed so that the wheel and tangents can be seen. (*Musikinstrumenten Museum, Berlin, 4087*)

trembling bridge, like that of the tromba marina, to add a buzzing rasping sound which was not always required. Tangents were fixed to each key bar and when the player pressed a key inwards towards the box, the tangents moved sideways against the chanterelles, stopping them at whatever length was correct for that key. The instrument was always played with its back against the player's body and the keys on the lower side so that when a key was released by the finger, the tangent would fall away

from the string. Obviously, only the strings that were accessible to the tangents could produce a melody, and it is important, when looking at the number of strings running through the tangent box, to count the number of rows of tangents as well; three strings but two rows of tangents means that one of the drones is inside the box. The melody strings were tuned in unison so that the one reinforced the other, and the drones in unisons, octave and fifth to provide an accompaniment the same as that of the bagpipe.

Many hurdy-gurdies were much more ornate than the one shown in the plate, for as with all fashionable instruments, the more the irrelevant ornamentation, the higher the value of the instrument in the eyes of those who were not serious players.

The Guitar and the Lute

The other most popular instrument of the French court was the guitar (plate 91), so often seen in the paintings of Watteau and his school (plate XIII). It was now always made with a flat back and usually with a fair amount of decoration on the belly and the body. It seems to have been used to entertain the court at *fêtes champêtres*, picnics and other alfresco pleasures in the gardens of Versailles, but on the whole the plucked string instruments were much less often used in formal music than before. They were popular for domestic music and entertainment; Schubert would accompany his own songs on the guitar, and there is some evidence that Beethoven was fond of the mandolin. Mozart scored for the mandolin in *Don Giovanni* to accompany a serenade (only too often replaced in the opera house by a pizzicato violin to avoid the expense of employing an extra player just for the one aria), and Vivaldi wrote concertos for it in the previous period.

It might be said that the ordinary lute was completely extinct, were it not that there are some instruments extant with a maker's label of this period. One must never forget that however important the main streams of music appear to the historian, the musicians, and especially the amateur musicians as well as the professionals in small towns and in the more isolated areas, went on playing the music they liked on whatever instruments they preferred, and there have always been makers willing to make whatever instruments the customers demanded. Certainly the bass lutes, theorbo and chitarrone were still widely used for accompaniments and to provide the bass for small ensembles. There are pictures of these at the French court and elsewhere, and a particularly interesting picture (see frontispiece) shows Mozart playing the violin accompanied by his sister playing a very small square piano, which would have a weak tone in the bass, and by his father on a bass lute, which would provide a good solid bass part, and such a use of the bass lute remained quite common.

Plate 91 Guitar by Colin, Paris, *c.* 1760. Five double courses. (*Donaldson Collection, 167, Royal College of Music, London*)

The English Guitar

One of the most popular instruments of the Eliza-
bethan period and the seventeenth century, the
cittern, made a dramatic reappearance in the latter
part of the eighteenth century, but in a new guise.
The cittern, which has been described in Chapter I,
had a body which tapered in depth, being deeper
from front to back at the top and thinner at the bottom, and the back of the neck was cut away at one
side, leaving it thinner, to make it easier for the
fingers to reach the strings. The new instrument had
an ordinary neck like a guitar and the body also
differed from that of the cittern in that, although it
looked much the same from the front, the depth did

not taper and the front and the back remained the
same distance apart from top to bottom. The depth
of the body was greater than that of the cittern so
that the English guitar had a deeper resonance box.
The stringing was different and it was simpler than
the old French cittern tuning and fretting. The wire
strings were in multiple courses, and although the
earlier instruments such as the lower on plate 92
had normal tuning pegs, many instruments, like the
upper on the plate, used Preston's invention of
machine tuning by a watch-key which turned a
threaded rod along which was drawn a hook to
which the string was attached.

These instruments had been popular in Germany,

116

and in France under the name of *cistre* (which is also the French for cittern), before they appeared in England. A problem is the date and source of their introduction in Portugal where they are still used and where they are called *guitarra*; the instrument that we call the guitar is the *viola* in Portuguese, and it is only in Portuguese and in English that this late form of the cittern has a name of its own. The question, to which we do not yet know the answer, is whether this was a Portuguese instrument, which spread over the rest of Europe as the waisted guitar had done from Spain many years before, or whether the English instrument had been carried to Portugal by the English merchants in the cork and the port trades and was adopted as the national form of the guitar. The evidence at present available suggests that the course of development and transmission was from France to England and thence to Portugal; but it is still uncertain whether the instrument originated in France or travelled thither from Germany or elsewhere, for instance from Sicily where the flat-backed mandolin is of similar shape.

In France, Germany and Sweden bass instruments of this type, under such names as *archicistre* or *théorbe* (plate 93), were popular, with a crooked neck like that of the theorbo carrying a second set of pegs for the bass strings. Both treble and bass instruments often had holes drilled through the fingerboard and the neck between the frets so that a capotasto could be fitted. This device was not new at this period and it was, and still is, a popular and useful way of allowing a guitarist to finger in a familiar way even when playing in a new and unfamiliar key. A bar is fixed over the strings, pressing them all to the fingerboard behind whichever fret is chosen, as on the upper guitar on plate 92, and the player then treats that fret as though it were the nut terminating the string length, and fingers the next fret as though it were the first fret on the full-length neck and thus transposes into the new key without any mental effort. Such a device is particularly useful when accompanying a singer, the range of whose voice can be easily accommodated in this way. The modern capotasto is tied or clamped round the neck; on the eighteenth century instrument, the neck was drilled and the capotasto held in position by a wing-nut on a threaded rod which passed through a hole in the neck.

The English guitar was designed with the genteel lady in mind, and some of these customers found it indelicate, and perhaps bad for their fingernails, to pluck the strings, which suggests that the wire strings were plucked with the fingers rather than with a plectrum. To spare them, various devices operated by piano-type keys were attached. Smith's Patent Box, which is fitted on the upper guitar on plate 92, for which no patent was ever taken out, could be clamped on to the instrument so that hammers within the box struck the strings when the appropriate key was depressed. Other types of keybox, such as that patented by Clauss, were built into the guitar with keys that rose through holes in the soundboard.

The popularity of the instrument in London, especially with the lady amateur, was such that harpsichord makers became seriously worried; far

Plate 93 Archicistre (arch-guitar) by Sébastien Renault and François Chatelain, Paris, 1785. 7 courses on the fingerboard, 4 double and 3 single, and 5 basses. (*Conservatoire Museum, Paris, C.260*)

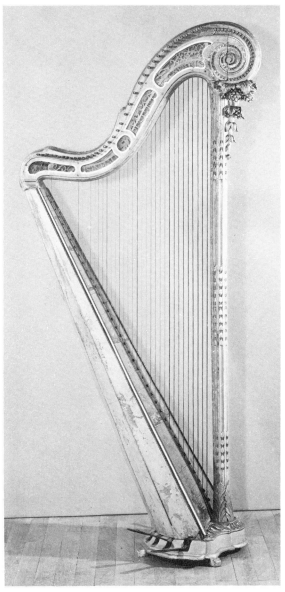

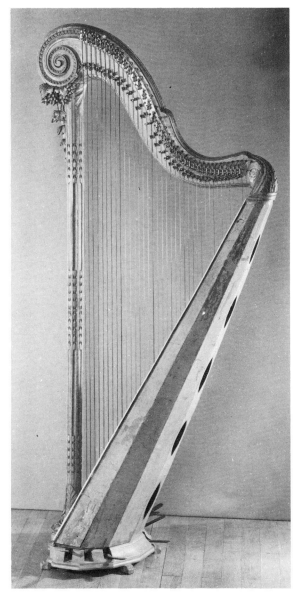

Plate 94 Pedal harp by Cousineau père et fils, Paris, late 18th century, showing both sides of the instrument. (*Musikinstrumenten Museum, Berlin, 2385*)

too many people were selling their harpsichords and buying English guitars instead. The story is told that Kirckman hit upon the solution—he gave away a quantity of English guitars to seamstresses, ladies who combined their skill at sewing with a rather older profession, with the result that the respectable ladies of fashion immediately discarded their guitars and returned to the harpsichord.

The Harp

The harp was a fashionable instrument in the latter part of the eighteenth century, probably because it looks so attractive standing in a room and because it is ideally designed to set off the beauty and the grace of the young ladies of the household. The harp was built with a set of pedals, each of which operated the mechanism that raised the pitch of all the strings of one note name (plate 94), one pedal operating on all the C strings, another on all the D strings and so forth. Sometimes an eighth pedal opened or closed a set of shutters in the back of the sound box, thus increasing or decreasing the volume. Various types of mechanism were in use. Sebastian Erard had already developed his *fourchettes*, a pair of pins set in a wheel, which, when the wheel was turned by the pedal, gripped the string to shorten its length at the appropriate point to raise the pitch by a semitone; he went on early in the nineteenth century to fit a second row of fourchettes, and a second notch to hold the pedal down, and thus invented the double-action harp which is still in use today. Not all players would be sufficiently up to date to use Erard's system, and while the hook harp was completely out of date except as a folk instrument in country districts, where it can still sometimes be found, the earlier pedal-operated harps such as Nadermann's with its *crochets* were still being made and used (plate 64), and Cousineau's mechanism with the *béquilles* (plate 95) was more often used than the newer system of Erard. The béquilles were a pair of small crutches that turned, one clockwise and the other anti-clockwise, towards the string to grip it and shorten its sounding length.

Keyboard Instruments

One thing that is often forgotten is the amount of domestic music-making that went on at all periods before the present surfeit of canned, piped and broadcast music saved people the trouble of learning how to produce their own music, and the amount of activity by instrument makers and publishers that furnished it with its material. There was no law of copyright and throughout the eighteenth century, as in earlier periods, anybody was free to produce editions of anybody else's music for whatever combination of instruments that he thought would sell, from Handel's 'Hallelujah Chorus' arranged for two flutes to a Haydn symphony arranged for harp. Mozart wrote to his father complaining that he was spending all his time producing an arrangement of his new opera for wind octet, simply so that he could get it to a publisher and earn some money before somebody else pirated it, although, since Mozart had also been known to write out the music of other composers so that he could perform or publish it for his own profit, he was hardly in a position to complain. A great deal of the music arranged in this way was designed for the amateur and domestic market and then, as now, the most important instruments

for domestic music-making were the keyboards.

The Clavichord

The clavichord reached its final form in the middle of the century; the instruments were large, often bigger than the square pianos that succeeded them, fully chromatic from end to end, fully fret-free, and with a separate pair of strings for each tangent and often with a third string at 4' pitch for each note of the bass (plate XIV). This extra string at the octave above the main strings was probably necessary because the greater tension of the fret-free instruments reduced the volume they could produce. This was

Plate 95 Detail of the béquilles which grip the string to raise the pitch by a semitone on the Cousineau harp in plate 94.

the instrument for which composers such as Carl Philipp Emanuel Bach wrote and which he had in mind when he was writing his famous textbook on playing keyboard instruments. It was the most important domestic keyboard instrument of its day, for although it was bigger than in the past, it was still much smaller and cheaper than a harpsichord or an organ and, as at all periods in its life, which was longer than that of any other keyboard instrument save the organ, it was capable of the fullest expression. Able to sustain its notes and to grow softer or louder as the player wished, it could give the illusion of swelling on any note by use of the *Bebung*, the vertical vibrato of the finger on the key, which was also used to smooth the transition of one note into the next in legato passages, an affect for which C. P. E. Bach was himself famous. The only country in which the clavichord seems to have been comparatively little used is Britain.

The Harpsichord

The changing character of musical taste and the rise to popularity of the pianoforte, which derives its name from the ability to play both piano and forte and all gradations of intermediate volume, forced harpsichord makers to go to extraordinary lengths to try to turn the harpsichord into an expressive instrument, a role quite foreign to its nature. The harpsichord excels at clarity of line and definition of attack, and its sound blends better than that of any other keyboard instrument with a small body of string instruments. It is by its nature incapable of any crescendo or diminuendo and, although the player can make it play moderately loudly or softly by using one or more choirs of strings, it cannot play sufficiently loudly to balance a large group of strings, nor can the player, by striking the keys more strongly, compel it to play more loudly than its maker intended, as he can with the piano. The English makers

Plate 96   Square piano by Johann Christoph Zumpe, London, 1767. GG-f³ without GG sharp. Zumpe's first action and the earliest known English pianoforte of normal compass. Two handstops to raise the dampers for sustaining. (*Victoria & Albert Museum, London, W.27–1928*)

of the harpsichord in the late eighteenth century, a time when it was already dying out in the rest of Europe, endeavoured to prolong its life by attaching such mechanical devices as the machine stop, an equivalent of the organ piston which will bring in a group of preselected stops, and the swell.

The swell box had been fitted to the organ from the early years of the century and its principle, the use of wooden shutters that could be gradually opened, so letting out more sound, was applied to the lyrichord, a keyboard instrument sounded by wheels, by its inventor Roger Plenius in 1747, and to the harpsichord by both the great London makers, Burkat Shudi and Jacob Kirckman. Shudi took out a patent on the Venetian Swell in 1769 but it is by no means clear whether such a device was new at that date, nor is it clear whether it was Shudi or Kirckman who first fitted a swell to a harpsichord. Two types were used, the nag's head and the Venetian. The nag's head swell was a lid in two pieces, one of which remained closed while the other, the one next to the bent side and the short straight side on the treble end of the keyboard and thus looking somewhat like a horse's head, opened when a pedal was depressed to let out more sound. The Venetian swell (plate XV) was rather more complicated; it consisted of a series of slats, like a horizontal Venetian blind, which, when closed, formed an inner lid and which, again when impelled by a pedal, each opened along its treble edge, being hinged along the bass edge, to let out the sound. Although the swell was constructed so that the harpsichord could produce a crescendo, the maximum volume with the swell open was much the same as it had been before, and when the swell was closed, the instrument was much quieter than before; the harpsichord had thus gained in expression in a way that was not natural to it, but only by sometimes playing more softly than it had done in the past.

However, the number of harpsichords dating from the last quarter of the century (the last known date of manufacture in London is 1800) indicates that a sufficiency of English musicians were old-fashioned enough to prefer the harpsichord to the piano, and it cannot be denied that these big harpsichords by Shudi and Broadwood and by the Kirckmans are superb instruments. Despite their quality and despite the fact that most late eighteenth century keyboard music was published as being for Harpsichord or Pianoforte, the new styles in music were inherently unsuitable for the harpsichord and it was not long before it vanished from the scene.

The Fortepiano

Silbermann's improved mechanism, which was soon to be employed so extensively by English makers that when it was reimported to the Continent it became known as the English action, made the piano a much more reliable, responsive and efficient instrument than it had been. The main cause of its rise was, of course, the changing style of the music, for everything in the new style that was foreign to the nature of the harpsichord was built into the character of the piano. Here was an instrument that could play loudly or softly at the touch of a finger. Because the key of a piano throws a hammer at the string, a light touch on the key will throw it gently, producing a quiet sound, and a strong touch will throw it hard, producing a loud sound; the fortepiano, as it was known in Britain, could play forte or piano as the player desired. This suited the new styles of music so well that piano making spread rapidly and, as pianos became more widely available, so did piano playing. One of the first to introduce it into Britain was Johann Christian Bach, the youngest son of J. S. Bach, and his music proved so popular that a number of piano makers, one of the better known of whom was Johann Zumpe, set up their workshops in London to satisfy the demand for the new instruments. The pianos that Zumpe produced were small instruments, as can be seen in plates 96 and 97, no larger than clavichords and, in fact, smaller than some of the large clavichords that have survived, especially the Swedish ones. It is thought that Zumpe may have been a workman in Shudi's harpsichord making firm, but it is known that many German piano makers came to London to escape the wars that ravaged Germany in the middle of the century and it is possible that Zumpe may have been one of them. What is certain is that his were at first the most popular pianos in London, so popular that many were exported to the Continent where they were widely copied, especially in France.

One of Shudi's apprentices, one who had sufficient sense to marry his master's daughter and thus become a partner in the firm, was John Broadwood,

Plate 97   Detail of the
keyboard, strings, hammers and
dampers of the Zumpe square
piano in plate 96.

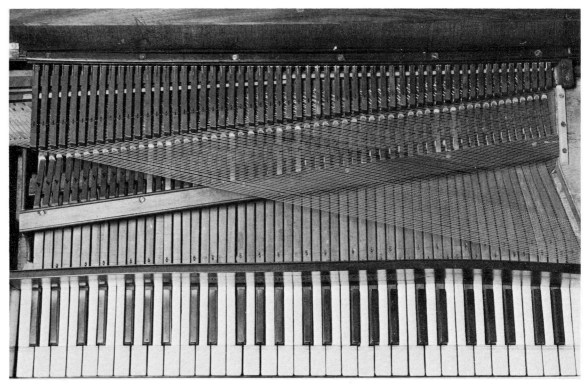

and although he began his life as a harpsichord maker (there are a number of surviving harpsichords marked Shudi and Broadwood), he became one of the leading English makers of fortepianos. His early models (plate 98) are externally almost identical with his single manual harpsichords, but internally there are considerable differences. The action of the piano, striking the strings with hammers, was comparatively ineffective on strings as light as those fitted to the harpsichord, and heavier strings, three to each note, were fitted to the piano, greatly increasing the strain on the frame. As a result, the internal barring and the strutting were strengthened. The increase in the total string tension was such that the gap through which the hammers rose, between the soundboard and the wrest plank in which the tuning pins were set, was more likely to close up under the strain than it had been on the harpsichord. Broadwood introduced metal bracing at this point on his pianos, as can be seen in plate 98, to prevent this happening. It was only in England, old-fashioned in musical taste as ever, that the same man could make harpsichords for much of his career (the last with the Broadwood name date from the 1790s) and supply

Beethoven with a piano before his career was over. Beethoven's piano was a later model, but the piano shown in plate 98 is the same model as those that Haydn played while he was in London, one of which he ordered and took back to Vienna with him.

In Vienna, a new model of the fortepiano had been developed (plate 99), best exemplified by the work of the Stein family, and this was the type of piano used by Mozart and which led to the second generation of piano players and composers. Mozart had, as a child in London, studied with J. C. Bach and perhaps played on a Zumpe square piano like that illustrated in plate 96, a typical instrument of the first generation. Mozart's own music demanded a greater brilliance and virtuosity than J. C. Bach's, and this was aided by the Viennese action, which was more suited than Zumpe's to this type of music. It was this type of piano for which the great Viennese school of composers wrote—Mozart, Haydn, Schubert and the early Beethoven—and this is the instrument which is being revived for the authentic performance of their keyboard music and which is today usually referred to as a fortepiano. The sound is surprisingly close to that of a harpsichord, though

Plate 98   Grand pianoforte by John Broadwood, London, 1794, FF–c⁴. An identical instrument was ordered by Haydn while in London. (*Colt Clavier Collection, Bethersden, Kent*)

of course with the greater range of expression natural to the instrument.

The sound of the fortepiano blends well with string instruments so that it is not surprising that it took over the responsibility for providing the keyboard continuo. When Haydn came to London for Salomon's concerts, it was announced that he would preside at the pianoforte; when Beethoven wrote his piano concertos, the piano part included figured basses in the tuttis. The continuo survived for a long time after what most modern performers think of as its end, around the middle of the century, and authentic performances of all eighteenth century music, right up to the end of the century and perhaps even into the nineteenth century, should include the use of a continuo instrument. The problem is determining what it should play.

The sound of the fortepiano was totally different from that of the modern piano; much quieter of course, but with a clarity, especially in the bass, which is unknown today. We tend to blame composers for writing bass parts in their piano music which sound blurred and confused, but these sound clear enough when they are played on the pianos of their own period. The fault lies in the modern piano, not with the composer.

One of the many things that we do not know about original performances is the extent to which the special effects, which were often built into the pianos, were used. As well as the two pedals to which we are accustomed today (the *una corda*, which shifts the action over a short distance so that the hammers strike on only one or two of the strings instead of on all three, and the sustaining pedal, often wrongly called the loud pedal, which lifts the dampers so that the notes continue to sound after the key has been released), there were often several more, the exact number and their order varying from one maker to another and from instrument to instrument. One or more, for each pedal often controlled only part of the compass, provided an imitation of the bassoon by touching a strip of parchment to the strings and so producing a buzzing tone. There were other ways than the *una corda* of decreasing the volume, sometimes by pressing to the strings a thin cloth or a set of leather pads such as had been fitted as the buff stop on the harpsichord. Another brought in the Turkish effects of drum and triangle or bells, and others might bring in either the drum or the triangle alone. Apart from the *alla Turca* pieces written by various composers such as Mozart and Beethoven, and occasional original indications of *una corda* or of the use of the sustaining pedal, we have no idea of the extent to which these devices were employed.

The Musical Glasses and the Glass Harmonica

A particular favourite among the travelling virtuosi of the latter half of the eighteenth century was the musical glasses, a set of wine glasses or glass bowls (plate 100) tuned to different pitches. These were played by rubbing a moistened finger round the rim, as can be done with any good quality wine glass, to produce a clear singing ring of great penetration. The need to keep the finger moistened to the correct extent, neither too wet nor too dry, must have been one of the problems of playing the instrument; another was the continual friction of the edge of the glass on the fingertips, which, combined with the singing whine of the glasses, sent many of its practitioners mad.

The American philosopher, inventor, revolutionary and statesman, Benjamin Franklin, invented an improved version in the 1760s. The glass harmonica (plate 101) consisted of a set of glass bowls fixed concentrically on a spindle, an adaptation that had a number of advantages. For one thing it could be set in a trough containing a little water, enough to keep the edges of the bowls and the fingers moist. For another, the spindle could be turned by a treadle like that on an old-fashioned sewing machine, which meant that the fingers could simply be held to the revolving bowls instead of having to circle the rim of each separate bowl or glass. For a third, and musically the most important, because each bowl was set into the next larger in size, with only a centimetre or so of rim projecting, the hands could span and touch a number of bowls simultaneously. The player of the old musical glasses could sound no more than two at a time, but the player of the glass harmonica could play chords as freely as on any keyboard instrument. The number surviving of so fragile an instrument attests its popularity, and that it had serious musical possibilities and qualities is suggested by the number of eminent composers who wrote for it, though it may have been the fact that

they were needy as well as eminent that induced them to do so. Every composer of the day would execute any commission that brought a fee, whether it were to write for musical glasses, for musical clocks, or for any other instrument. Mozart's *Adagio and Rondo* for glass harmonica and other instruments is one of the most beautiful of his shorter chamber works, and no instrument for which such music exists can be dismissed as an amateur's toy and unworthy of revival today.

So we draw to the end of the eighteenth century, a period which saw great changes in musical styles and in the instruments which performed the music, just as it saw great changes in society and in politics, with revolutions in France and in America as well as in industry and in commerce. At the beginning of the seventeenth century, the orchestra had consisted of a handful of strings with plucked string and keyboard continuo; now it was of a size that we would recognise in a concert hall today, with a dozen wind

Plate 99 Fortepiano by Mathaeus Heilman, Mainz, 1775, FF-f³, such as was used by Mozart in Vienna. (*Colt Clavier Collection, Bethersden, Kent*)

Plate 100 Musical glasses, anonymous, England, c. 1800. c²-f⁴, fully chromatic, with extra bowls for water to moisten the fingers. (*Dr. W. M. Meier*)

instruments and timpani, and a considerable body of bowed strings, a group that was large enough that there was no real need for a keyboard continuo, although it remained the custom for such a player to help to hold the orchestra together even when the leading violinist was directing the performance.

We have seen many instruments arrive on the musical scene; some flourished for a few years, some for a century or so, but all of the instruments playing in the orchestra for which Beethoven wrote his first symphony in 1800 are still playing in the symphony orchestras that we hear today. They have changed, of course, and these changes remain to be charted and described in the next volume of this series. It is a characteristic of music that it does change, that every generation has its own musical style, sometimes based on that of the generation which went before it, sometimes rebelling against and contrasting with the music of the previous generation. Similarly, every generation has its preferred sonority, its own ideal for the instrumental sound that best suits its music, its social conditions and the rooms and the halls in which its music is played. The musical instruments are designed to produce this favoured sonority, they are constructed to be able to play the types of music that are in fashion, but their design and construction are also controlled by the levels of technology reached by the society in which they are made. Sometimes inventions come before their time, such as Cristo-

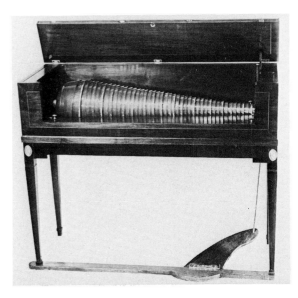

Plate 101 Glass harmonica, anonymous, *c.* 1800. (*Musikinstrumenten Museum, Berlin, 812*)

fori's invention of the pianoforte; sometimes we see an instrument relegated to a simpler role than in an earlier period for lack of an invention which would enable it to lead a fuller musical life, as with the orchestral trumpet in the latter part of the eighteenth century. Music can proceed no further than technology will permit and technology alone can never gain acceptance for an instrument for which there is no musical use. The two grow together: music stands on technology's shoulders and technology can provide only what music will accept.

Acknowledgements

First and foremost I must thank my wife, to whom this book is
dedicated, for as well as providing constant support and encouragement
and making many suggestions which have led to improvements
throughout the text, she has undertaken the whole task of obtaining the
photographs illustrating this book. As always, I owe a debt of gratitude
to all my colleagues and friends who have so patiently answered my
questions and who have allowed me to use the knowledge, references
and information they have provided. I am more than grateful to all
those people and institutions that have allowed me to photograph their
instruments, and to those that have provided me with photographs; were
it not for their willingness to spend the time in taking all the photographs
requested, it would have been impossible to produce a book such as this.

Bibliography

Abbreviations: GSJ—The Galpin Society Journal; EM—Early Music; FoMRHIQ—Fellowship of Makers & Restorers of Historical Instruments Quarterly

Abbott, Djilda & Ephraim Segerman. 'Catline Strings', *FoMRHIQ* 12, comm. 137 (1978)

Altenburg, Johann Ernst. *Versuch einer Anleitung zur heroisch-musikalischen Trompeter- und Pauker-Kunst* (Halle, 1795; English translation by Edward Tarr, Brass Press, Nashville, 1974)

Arbeau, Thoinot. *Orchésographie* (Langres, 1588; facsimile Minkoff, Geneva, 1972)

Bach, Carl Philipp Emanuel. *Versuch über die wahre Art das Clavier zu Spielen* (Berlin, 1753 & 1762; English translation by William J. Mitchell, Cassell, 1949)

Baines, Anthony C. *Bagpipes* (Pitt Rivers Museum, Oxford, 1960)

——. *Brass Instruments, their History and Development* (Faber & Faber, 1976)

——. *European and American Musical Instruments* (Batsford, 1966)

——. *Non-Keyboard Instruments* (Victoria & Albert Museum, Catalogue of Musical Instruments, vol. 2, H.M.S.O., 1968)

——. 'James Talbot's MS I—Wind Instruments', *GSJ* 1 (1948)

——. *Woodwind Instruments and their History* (3rd ed, Faber & Faber, 1967)

——. (ed). *Musical Instruments Through the Ages* (2nd ed, Penguin and Faber & Faber, 1966)

Barbour, J. Murray. *Tuning and Temperament* (Michigan U.P., 1951; reprint Da Capo, New York, 1972)

Bate, Philip. *The Flute* (Benn, 1969)

——. *The Oboe* (2nd ed. Benn, 1962)

Bessaraboff, Nicholas. *Ancient European Musical Instruments* (Museum of Fine Arts, Boston, 1941)

Blades, James. *Percussion Instruments and their History* (2nd ed, Faber & Faber, 1975)

—— & Jeremy Montagu. *Early Percussion Instruments* (O.U.P., 1976)

Bonanni, Filippo. *Gabinetto Armonico* (Rome, 1723; illustrations only (with new text) reprinted Dover, New York, 1964)

Boyden, David. *Catalogue of The Hill Collection of Musical Instruments in the Ashmolean Museum, Oxford* (O.U.P., 1969)

——. *The History of Violin Playing from its origins to 1761* (O.U.P., 1965)

Buchner, Alexandr. *Musical Instruments: an Illustrated History* (2nd ed of *Musical Instruments Through the Ages*, Octopus, 1973)

Byrne, Maurice. 'The Church Band at Swalcliffe', *GSJ* 17 (1964)

——. 'The Goldsmith-Trumpet-Makers of the British Isles', *GSJ* 19 (1966)

Clagget, Charles. Patent Specification no. 1664, August 15th 1788

Cocks, W. A. 'James Talbot's MS III—Bagpipes', *GSJ* 5 (1952)

Cudworth, Charles. 'John Marsh's Advice to Young Composers of Instrumental Music', *GSJ* 18 (1965)

Dahlqvist, Reine. *The Keyed Trumpet* (Brass Press, Nashville, 1975)

Dart, Thurston. 'The Mock Trumpet', *GSJ* 6 (1953)

Diderot, Denis & Jean d'Alembert. *Encyclopédie* (Paris, 1751 etc; reprint of Lutherie plates as *The Manufacture of Musical Instruments*, Picton, Chippenham, 1975)

Donington, Robert. 'James Talbot's MS II—Bowed Strings', *GSJ* 3 (1950)

Early Music, 1973- . Published quarterly by O.U.P.

Fantini, Girolamo. *Modo per Imparare a sonare di Tromba* (Frankfurt, 1638; facsimile Brass Press, Nashville, 1972)

Farmer, Henry George. *Handel's Kettledrums* (Hinrichsen, 1960)

Fellowship of Makers & Restorers of Historical Instruments Quarterly, 1975- . Issued quarterly from 7 Pickwick Road, London SE21

Galpin, Francis W. *Old English Instruments of Music* (4th ed, Methuen, 1965)

The Galpin Society Journal, 1948- . Published annually, for the study of musical instruments, from 116 Tenison Road, Cambridge

Geminiani, Francesco. *The Art of Playing on the Violin* (1751; facsimile, O.U.P., nd)

Gill, Donald. 'James Talbot's MS V—Plucked Strings' *GSJ* 15 (1962)

——. *Wire-strung Plucked Instruments Contemporary with the Lute* (Lute Society Booklet no. 3, Richmond, 1977)

Grove's Dictionary of Music & Musicians (5th ed, Macmillan, 1954)

Halfpenny, Eric. Articles on English and French

Hautboys, *GSJ* 2, 6 & 8 (1949, 1953 & 1955)

——. 'Early British Trumpet Mouthpieces', *GSJ* 20 (1967)

——. 'Technology of a Bass Recorder', *GSJ* 15, 1962

——. 'The "Tenner Hoboy" ', *GSJ* 5, 1952

——. 'Two Rare Transverse Flutes', *GSJ* 13, 1960

——. 'William Bull and the English Baroque Trumpet', *GSJ* 15 (1962)

——. 'William Shaw's "Harmonic Trumpet" ', *GSJ* 13 (1960)

Hotteterre, Jacques ('Le Romain'). *Principes de la Flute Traversiere*, (Estienne Roger, Amsterdam, 1728; facsimile Bärenreiter, Kassel, 1958)

Kinsky, Georg. *Geschichte der Musik in Bildern* (Leipzig, 1929; also published in English, French and Italian)

Krickeberg, Dieter & Wolfgang Rauch. *Katalog der Blechblasinstrumente* (Musikinstrumenten-Museum, Berlin, 1976)

Mace, Thomas. *Musick's Monument* (1676; facsimile Centre National de la Recherche Scientifique, Paris, 1958)

Mahillon, Victor-Charles. *Catalogue descriptif et analytique du Musée Instrumental du Conservatoire Royal de Musique de Bruxelles* (Ghent and Brussels, for the Museum, 1880-1922; reprint announced 1978)

Marsh, John. 'Advice to Young Composers of Instrumental Music', *GSJ* 18 (1965)

Marvin, Bob. 'Report on FoMRHI Seminar no. 2', *FoMRHIQ* 7, comm. 55 (1977)

Meeùs, Nicolas. 'Renaissance Transposing Keyboard Instruments', *FoMRHIQ* 6 & 7, comms. 45 & 57 (1977)

Mersenne, Marin. *Harmonie Universelle* (Cramoisy, Paris, 1636; facsimile Centre National de la Recherche Scientifique, Paris, 1963)

Monk, Christopher. 'First Steps Towards Playing the Cornett', *EM* 3 nos. 2 & 3 (1975)

Montagu, Jeremy. 'Choosing Brass Instruments', *EM* 4 no. 1 (1976)

——. *Making Early Percussion Instruments* (O.U.P., 1976)

——. *The World of Medieval & Renaissance Musical Instruments* (David & Charles, Newton Abbot; Overlook, Woodstock, 1976)

Mould, Charles. 'James Talbot's MS VIII—Harpsichord', *GSJ* 21 (1968)

Mozart, Leopold. *Versuch einer gründlichen Violinschule* (Augsburg 1756; English translation by Editha Knocker, 1951)

Otto, Irmgard & Olga Adelmann. *Katalog der Streichinstrumente* (Musikinstrumenten-Museum, Berlin, 1975)

Pegge, R. Morley. *The French Horn* (Benn, 1960)

——. 'Serpent', *Grove* 5th ed, (Macmillan, 1954)

Pepys, Samuel. *Diaries*, 1659-69 (numerous editions)

Potter, Richard. Patent Specification no. 1499, October 28th 1785

Praetorius, Michael. *Syntagmatis Musici 2: de Organographia* (Wolfenbüttel, 1619; facsimile Bärenreiter, Kassel, 1958)

Prynne, Michael. 'James Talbot's MS IV—Plucked Strings—The Lute Family', *GSJ* 14 (1961)

Quantz, Johann Joachim. *Versuch einer Anweisung die Flöte traversière zu spielen* (Voss, Berlin, 1752)

Rendall, F. Geoffrey. *The Clarinet* (3rd ed, Benn, 1971)

Rimmer, Joan. 'James Talbot's MS VI—Harps', *GSJ* 16 (1963)

——. 'The Morphology of the Triple Harp' *GSJ* 18 (1965)

Russell, Raymond. *The Harpsichord and Clavichord* (Faber & Faber, 1959)

——. *Keyboard Instruments* (Victoria & Albert Museum, Catalogue of Musical Instruments, vol. 1, H.M.S.O., 1968)

Sachs, Curt. *Handbuch der Musikinstrumentenkunde* (Breitkopf & Härtel, Leipzig, 1930)

——. *The History of Musical Instruments* (Norton, New York, 1940)

——. *Sammlung alter Musikinstrumente bei der staatlichen Hochschule für Musik zu Berlin* (Berlin, 1922)

Sauerlandt, Max. *Die Musik in fünfjahrhunderten der Europäischen Malerei* (Langewiesche, Leipzig, 1922)

Schlosser, Julius. *Die Sammlung alter Musikinstrumente, Kunsthistorisches Museum in Wien* (Vienna, 1920; reprint Olms, Hildesheim, 1974)

Talbot, James. *Manuscript* (Christ Church Library, Oxford, Music Ms 1187). *See:* Baines, Cocks, Donington, Gill, Mould, Prynne, Rimmer

Wachsmann, K. P. 'A Drum from Seventeenth Century Africa', *GSJ* 23 (1970)

Williams, Peter. *The European Organ 1450-1850* (Batsford, 1966)

Index

1. 2. 3. Violn de Gamba.   4. Viol Baftarda.   5. Italianifche Lyra de bracio.